More than
1,000 *Sunan*
Every Day & Night

Second Edition: June 2006

Supervised by:

ABDUL MALIK MUJAHID

© **Maktaba Dar-us-Salam, 2006**

King Fahd National Library Cataloging-in-Publication Data

Maktaba Dar-us-Salam, Research & Compilation Department
  More than 1.000 Sunan every day & night. / Maktaba
Dar-us-Salam Research & Compilation Department - Riyadh, 2006
128 p ; 14 x 21 cm
     ISBN: 9960-9801-7-0
  1-Al-Hadith - Literary collections 2- Invocation and award
I-Title
210 dc   1427/4202
   L.D. no. 1427/4202
   ISBN: 9960-9801-7-0

More than
1,000 *Sunan*
Every Day & Night

Based on the Arabic Book
Akthar Min Alf Sunnah
Fee- Al-Yawm Wa Al- Laylah

Compiled by
Shaykh Khaalid Al-Husaynaan

Translated by:
Aboo Ismaa'eel Munir

DARUSSALAM
GLOBAL LEADER IN ISLAMIC BOOKS
Riyadh • Jeddah • Al-Khobar • Sharjah
Lahore • London • Houston • New York

Revised Edition: 2010
Supervised by:
Abdul Malik Mujahid

HEAD OFFICE

P.O. Box: 22743, Riyadh 11416 K.S.A.Tel: 00966-1-4033962/4043432 Fax: 4021659
E-mail: darussalam@awalnet.net.sa, riyadh@dar-us-salam.com Website:www.darussalamksa.com

K.S.A. Darussalam Showrooms:

Riyadh
Olaya branch: Tel 00966-1-4614483 Fax: 4644945
Malaz branch: Tel 00966-1-4735220 Fax: 4735221
Suwaydi branch: Tel: 00966 1 4286641
Suwailam branch: Tel & Fax-1-2860422

- Jeddah
  Tel: 00966-2-6879254 Fax: 6336270
- Madinah
  Tel: 00966-04-8234446, 8230038
  Fax: 04-8151121
- Al-Khobar
  Tel: 00966-3-8692900 Fax: 8691551
- Khamis Mushayt
  Tel & Fax: 00966-072207055
* Yanbu Al-Bahr Tel: 0500887341 Fax: 04-3908027
- Al-Buraida Tel: 0503417156 Fax: 06-3696124

U.A.E
- Darussalam, Sharjah U.A.E
  Tel: 00971-6-5632623 Fax: 5632624
  Sharjah@dar-us-salam.com.

PAKISTAN
- Darussalam, 36 B Lower Mall, Lahore
  Tel: 0092-42-724 0024 Fax: 7354072
* Rahman Market, Ghazni Street,Urdu Bazar Lahore
  Tel: 0092-42-7120054 Fax: 7320703
- Karachi, Tel: 0092-21-4393936 Fax: 4393937
- Islamabad, Tel: 0092-51-2500237 Fax: 512281513

U.S.A
- Darussalam, Houston
  P.O Box: 79194 Tx 77279
  Tel: 001-713-722 0419 Fax: 001-713-722 0431
  E-mail: houston @dar-us-salam.com
- Darussalam, New York 486 Atlantic Ave, Brooklyn
  New York-11217, Tel: 001-718-625 5925
  Fax: 718-625 1511
  E-mail: darussalamny@hotmail.com

U.K
- Darussalam International Publications Ltd.
  Leyton Business Centre
  Unit-17, Etloe Road, Leyton, London, E10 7BT
  Tel: 0044 20 8539 4885 Fax:0044 20 8539 4889
  Website: www.darussalam.com
  Email: info@darussalam.com
- Darussalam International Publications Limited
  Regents Park Mosque, 146 Park Road
  London NW8 7RG Tel: 0044- 207 725 2246
  Fax: 0044 20 8539 4889

AUSTRALIA
- Darussalam: 153, Haldon St, Lakemba (Sydney)
  NSW 2195, Australia
  Tel: 0061-2-97407188 Fax: 0061-2-97407199
  Mobile: 0061-414580813 Res: 0061-2-97580190
  Email: abumuaaz@hotmail.com
- The Islamic Bookstore
  Ground Floor-165 Haldon Street
  Lakemba, NSW 2195, Australia
  Tel: 0061-2-97584040 Fax: 0061-2-97584030
  Email: info@islamicbookstore.com.au
  Web Site: www.islamicbookstore.com.au

CANADA
- Nasiruddin Al-Khattab
  2-3415 Dixie Rd, Unit # 505
  Mississauga
  Ontario L4Y 4J6, Canada
  Tel: 001-416-418 6619
- Islamic Book Service
  2200 South Sheridan way Mississauga, On
  L5J 2M4
  Tel: 001-905-403-8406 Ext. 218 Fax: 905-8409

FRANCE
- Editions & Librairie Essalam
  135, Bd de Ménilmontant- 75011 Paris
  Tél: 0033-01- 43 38 19 56/ 44 83
  Fax: 0033-01-43 57 44 31
  E-mail: essalam@essalam com·

MALAYSIA
- Darussalam
  Int'l Publishing & Distribution SDN BHD
  D-2-12, Setiawangsa 11, Taman Setiawangsa
  54200 Kuala Lumpur
  Tel: 03-42528200 Fax: 03-42529200
  Email: darussalam@streamyx.com
  Website: www.darussalam.com.my

SRI LANKA
- Darul Kitab 6, Nimal Road, Colombo-4
  Tel: 0094 115 358712 Fax: 115-358713

INDIA
- Islamic Books International
  54, Tandel Street (North)
  Dongri, Mumbai 4000 09, INDIA
  Tel: 0091-22-2373 4180
  E-mail: ibi@irf.net

SOUTH AFRICA
- Islamic Da'wah Movement (IDM)
  48009 Qualbert 4078 Durban,South Africa
  Tel: 0027-31-304-6883 Fax: 0027-31-305-1292
  E-mail: idm@ion.co.za

Contents

Foreword.. 7

A word from the Translator 9

Table of *Vowels*... 12

Taa Marbootah... 12

Table Of Consonants 12

Author's Introduction.. 13

Waking up... 17

Entering and leaving the toilet.................................... 18

Wudoo' 19

Benefits of observing these *Sunan* in *Wudoo'*:.......... 23

General words of advice from Imaam An-Nawawee:...... 23

Using a *Siwaak*... 24

Wearing shoes 25

Dressing and undressing..................................... 26

Entering and leaving the house........................... 27

Going to the *Masjid*... 29

The *Adhaan*.. 32

The *Iqaamah*... 35

Praying towards a *Sutrah*.................................. 36

Issues regarding the *Sutrah*............................. 36

Benefits of observing this *Sunnah*:................... 37

The Optional Prayers.. 38

The Night Prayer... 40

Things that help one to perform *Qiyaam Al-Layl*:...... 44

The *Witr* Prayer... 45

The *Fajr* Prayer... 47

Sitting after the *Fajr* Prayer............................. 49

Benefit of sitting in the *Masjid*:....................... 49

What is said during the Prayer.......................... 50

Points to note:... 53

Actions performed in the Prayer ... 54

Ar-Rukoo' ... 55

As-Sujood ... 56

Al-Jalsah ... 57

The final *Tashahhud* ... 58

Summary of actions in the prayer: ... 58

General words of advice from Ibn Al-Qayyim: ... 59

After the obligatory Prayers ... 60

Benefits of these *Adhkaar* : ... 64

Adhkaar of the morning and evening ... 66

Points to note: ... 76

Meeting people ... 77

Eating ... 81

Drinking ... 83

Performing voluntary Prayers at home ... 84

Leaving a gathering ... 86

From the benefits of implementing this *Sunnah* : ... 87

Ibn Al-Qayyim said the gathering of Muslims is of two types: ... 88

Making the correct intention ... 89

Important point: ... 89

Combining multiple acts of worship ... 90

Here are some examples: ... 90

Remembering Allah at all times ... 92

Points to note regarding *Dhikr* of Allah: ... 92

Reflecting on the blessings of Allah ... 95

Completing the Qur'an every month ... 97

Before going to sleep ... 98

Benefits of these *Sunan* when going to sleep: ... 104

Conclusion ... 106

Glossary of terms ... 107

Hadeeth References ... 112

FOREWORD

In the Name of Allah, the Most Gracious, the Most Merciful. May the praise of Allah, in the highest of assemblies, and His peace, safety and security, both in this world and the next, be on Muhammad (ﷺ), the best of mankind and the seal of the Prophets and Messengers.

The Prophetic sayings, actions and approvals contained in this booklet represent a good selection of the important matters necessary for every Muslim in their daily life.

It is hoped that if we implement these practices daily, doing so sincerely for the pleasure of Allah, we will have fulfilled the two conditions for the acceptability of acts of worship, namely: (i) *Al-Ikhlaas* (sincerity) and (ii) *Al-Mutaaba'ah* [adherence to the way of Prophet Muhammad (ﷺ)]. In this way, the true believer has hope of achieving the greatest success, *Al-Jannah*. O Allah! We ask of You *Al-Jannah* and seek refuge in you from *An- Naar*!

As I sat with the translator of this book, Aboo Ismaa'eel, reviewing this work in the library of a *Da'wah* centre in the city of Doha, Qatar, it brought back memories of those days when we sat with Aboo Safwaan, the translator of a similar work, *Hisn Al-Muslim*, in the library of the Prophet's *Masjid* in Al-Madeenah An-Nabaweeyah, reviewing similar issues.

I do not think any of the brothers involved in that work imagined the acclaim it would achieve.

However, success is from Allah and we hope that He will grant equal success to this work, make it a benefit to all those who read it and reward all those who have had anything to do with its realisation.

Indeed! He, the Mighty and the Majestic, is Generous and Able to do all things.

Abbur-Ra'uf Shakir

Doha, State of Qatar

Jumaadi Al-Awwal, 1426

A WORD FROM THE TRANSLATOR

All praise is for Allah, Lord of the worlds. May the *Salaah* and *Salaam* of Allah be on the final Prophet, Muhammad (ﷺ) his family, Companions and all those who follow them in righteousness, until the Day of Judgement.

Is it not amazing that in the course of a normal day, many of us are capable of practicing more than 1,000 *Sunan*? Surely, in clinging to the *Sunnah* is safety and security, as Imaam Maalik said:

> *The Sunnah is like the Ark of Noah-whoever embarks on it reaches salvation and whoever refuses is drowned.*

Before you is a short booklet containing statements and actions of the Prophet Muhammad (ﷺ) that are performed in a typical day – how many of these are part of our daily lives?

This work is the English-language translation of the Arabic booklet, *More Than 1,000 Sunan Every Day & Night,* complied by Shaykh Khaalid Husaynaan. He is a contemporary student of knowledge of our time who is preoccupied with reviving and following the *Sunnah* of Prophet Muhammad (ﷺ).

There are a few issues readers should be aware of. Firstly, all footnotes have been added by me and were not part of the original booklet.

Secondly, the order of some points has been changed from the original Arabic work. In all cases, however care has been exercised to ensure that the original intent and meaning has not been lost. Thirdly, all Arabic terms that are italicized have been defined in the Glossary Of Terms at the end. Finally, a clarification on the meaning of the title – the original Arabic booklet did not specifically mention 1,000 separate *Sunnah*; rather, the intent was that by performing the *Sunan* mentioned, with the frequency advised in the *Ahaadeeth*, one can end up fulfilling, during a single day and night, more than 1,000 *Sunan*.

No human effort is free from error and so I ask Allah, the Most Merciful, to forgive me for any inadvertent mistakes within this booklet.

Readers are encouraged to contact us if they notice any errors, whether in translation, grammar, use of sources or points discussed.

I ask Him, the Most High, by His beautiful Names and Attributes, that He guides us to the truth and that He purifies our intentions and gives me and those who participated in the translating and publishing of this book, whether in editing, checking, formatting or designing, a bountiful reward for striving in His way. May Allah make this of benefit for us in this Life and the Next.

Aboo Ismaa'eel Munir

Doha, State of Qatar

Jumaadi Al-Awwal, 1426

The transliteration system used in this book, is based on the one created by Dr. Bilal Philips. This system was preferred over others due to the ease with which English-speakers could understand it.

However, a few clarifying comments may be of assistance. Firstly, the Arabic definite article is written variously as '*Al*' or within the first letter of the following word, when pronunciation requires this, e.g. *Al-Rahmaan* is written and pronounced *Ar-Rahmaan*. Secondly, '*Shaddah*' (written ⁚), is represented by doubled consonants. Finally, '*Taa Marbootah*' (ة) is represented by '*H*' (e.g. *Salaah*). Readers should note, however, that in a construct phrase, the '*Taa Marbootah*' acquires a '*T*' sound (e.g. *Soorat Al-Baqarah*, not *Soorah Al-Baqarah*).

Table of *Vowels*

َ	a		اَ	aa
ُ	u		وُ	oo
ِ	i		يِ	ee

Taa Marbootah

ة	h		ة	t

Table Of Consonants

أ	'		ض	<u>d</u>
ب	b		ط	<u>t</u>
ت	t		ظ	<u>dh</u>
ث	th		ع	~
ج	j		غ	gh
ح	h		ف	f
خ	kh		ق	q
د	d		ك	k
ذ	dh		ل	l
ر	r		م	m
ز	z		ن	n
س	s		ه	h
ش	sh		و	w
ص	<u>s</u>		ي	y

AUTHOR'S INTRODUCTION

All praise is due to Allah, the Most Merciful the All-forgiving, the Most Generous, the All-Powerful, the Turner of hearts and sight, the Knower of the seen and the unseen. I continuously praise Him in the evening and the morning.

And I testify that Muhammad (ﷺ) is His chosen Messenger – may the peace and blessings of Allah be on him and on his family, his wives and Companions, all of whom are deserving of exaltation and reverence; a praise which is as everlasting as the day and the night.

To proceed: The most important thing that a Muslim can attend to and take care of in his daily life is acting according to the *Sunnah* of the Messenger ﷺ – whether it is the *Sunnah* of his *Harakaat* or *Sakanaat* the *Sunnah* of his actions – until the person organises his life in accordance to the *Sunnah* of the Messenger (ﷺ), from the morning to the evening.

Dhun-Nun Al-Masri said:

From the signs of one's love for Allah, is following His beloved Prophet's (ﷺ) actions, manners, commands and recommendations.

Allah (ﷺ) says:

﴿قُلْ إِن كُنتُمْ تُحِبُّونَ ٱللَّهَ فَٱتَّبِعُونِي يُحْبِبْكُمُ ٱللَّهُ وَيَغْفِرْ لَكُمْ ذُنُوبَكُمْ وَٱللَّهُ غَفُورٌ رَّحِيمٌ﴾

"Say; 'if you really love Allah then follow me and

Allah will love you and forgive your sins. And Allah is Oft-Forgiving, Most Merciful.' "

(*Aal-Imraan*, 3:31)

Hasan Al-Basri said:

The sign of their love (for Allah) is in their adherence to the Sunnah of His Prophet (ﷺ).

The rank of the believer is measured by his following of the Messenger (ﷺ) – he is higher and more exalted with Allah according to the extent of his practicing of the *Sunnah*.

For this reason I compiled this brief treatise – to revive the *Sunnah* of the Prophet (ﷺ) in the affairs of the Muslims; whether it is in their daily lives, worshipping, sleeping, eating and drinking, dealings with people, in their purification, entering and leaving of their homes, dressing and everything remaining of actions pertaining to *Harakaat* and *Sakanaat*.

It is interesting to note that if one of us lost some money, how concerned and worried we would be and how much effort we would exert in trying to find it.

But how many *Sunan* have we lost in our lives? Does this sadden us? Have we strived to revive them in our lives?

One of the problems we suffer from is that we have begun to value and admire the dinar and dirham more than the *Sunnah*. If people were told that whoever observed a *Sunnah* from the *Sunan* of the Prophet (ﷺ) would receive a certain amount of money, then you would certainly find them wanting to and striving to observe the *Sunnah* in all of their affairs, from the morning to the evening.

Why? Only because they would gain some money for every *Sunnah* practised.

How will this wealth benefit us when we are placed in our graves and the earth's dust is poured on us?

Allah (ﷻ) says:

﴿ بَلْ تُؤْثِرُونَ ٱلْحَيَوٰةَ ٱلدُّنْيَا ○ وَٱلْأَخِرَةُ خَيْرٌ وَأَبْقَىٰ ﴾

"Nay, you prefer the life of this world although the Hereafter is better and more lasting."

(Al-'Alaa,87:16-17)

The *Sunan* mentioned in this booklet are those things for which the one performing them is rewarded, while not being penalized for leaving them.

In addition, they are those things that are repeated in the day and night and are therefore within the capacity and ability of everyone to perform.

I found that it is possible for every person, if they strove to observe these daily *Sunan*, to perform no less than a thousand *Sunan* daily, covering all aspects of their lives.

This little booklet is noting more than clarification of the easiest way to implement these *Sunan*. If the Muslim sought to observe a thousand *Sunan* in the day and night, this would be approximately thirty thousand *Sunan* in a month.

Look at the person who is ignorant of these *Sunan* or who knows them but does not act by them: how much rank and reward does he forfeit for himself? Indeed he is truly deprived.

From the benefits of adhering to the *Sunnah* are:

☐ To reach the level of love – Love of Allah (ﷻ) for his believing slave.

☐ It is a means to compensate for any deficiency in the obligatory actions.

☐ It is a protection from falling into innovation.

☐ It indicates the exaltation of those things that represent the religion of Allah.[1]

By Allah, O *Ummah* of Islam, revive the *Sunan* of your Messenger (ﷺ) in all aspects of your lives, for the *Sunnah* is evidence of your complete love for the Messenger of Allah (ﷺ) and a sign of your sincerity in following him.

---

[1] To exalt, in this sense means to adhere to, or comply with something.

WAKING UP

1. Wipe the effects of sleep from the face with your hands:

   Imaam An-Nawawee and Ibn Hajar stated this wiping to be desirable based on the following:

   When the Messenger of Allah (ﷺ) woke up, he would sit up and rub away the effects of sleep from his face with his hand.

2. Say the supplication for waking up:

   «الْحَمْدُ للهِ الَّذِي أَحْيَانَا بَعْدَ مَا أَمَاتَنَا وَإِلَيْهِ النُّشُورُ»

   All praise is for Allah who gave us life after death (sleep) and to Him is the resurrection.

3. Use a *Siwaak*:

   When the Prophet (ﷺ) woke up from the night (sleep), he used to clean his mouth with a Siwaak.

4. Snuff water:

   When one of you wakes up from sleep, then snuff water three times. For indeed, Shaytaan spends the night in the upper part of his nose.

5. Wash both hands three times:

   When one of you wakes up from sleep, he must not dip his hand into a utensil until he washes it three times...

ENTERING AND LEAVING THE TOILET

1. Enter with the left foot and leave with the right.[1]

2. Supplicate when entering the toilet:

«اللَّهُمَّ إِنِّي أَعُوذُ بِكَ مِنَ الْخُبْثِ وَالْخَبَائِثِ»

O Allah, I seek refuge in You from Al-Khubth and Al-Khabaa'ith.[6]

3. Supplicate when leaving:

«غُفْرَانَكَ»

I ask You (Allah) for forgiveness.

People use the bathroom many times during the day and night. If they observe these *Sunan* for entering and leaving every time they go, they will fulfill two *Sunan* for entering and two *Sunan* for leaving.

Al-khubth and *Al-Khabaa'ith* – These are male and female devils.[2] In order to be protected by Allah from their evil, one should seek refuge from them when entering the toilet. The toilet is one of their places of abode.

---

[1] No evidence for entering with the left foot and leaving with the right was found. Therefore, it seems that general evidences indicating the use of the right for good and the left for the opposite have been used.

[2] There two opinions as to the meaning of *Al-khubth* and *Al-khabaa'ith*. The first is that it means, all evil and evildoers and the second is that it means, male and female devils. The *Shaykh* follows the latter opinion.

WUDOO'

1. Begin with *At-Tasmiyah* :

«بِسْمِ اللهِ»

In the Name of Allah.[1]

2. Wash both hands three times at the start of *Wudoo'*.

3. Rinse the mouth and snuff water into the nose before washing the face.

4. Expel water from the nose using the left hand:

He (ﷺ) washed his hands three times, then rinsed his mouth, snuffed water and blew it out.[2] Then he washed his face three times..

---

[1]   This is based on the *Hadeeth* of Aboo Hurayrah (ﷺ).

"There is no prayer for the person who has not performed Wudoo' and there is no Wudoo' for the one who does not mention the Name of Allah."

There is a difference of opinion amongst the scholars regarding this *Hadeeth*. Shaykh Al-Albaanee has mentioned the scholars who have declared this *Hadeeth* as good or authentic in *Irwaa Al-Ghaleel*, Volume 1, *Hadeeth* 81.

[2]   The use of the left hand was not explicitly mentioned in this *Hadeeth*, but there is a narration of Ad-Daarimee, 'Abd Khayr said, '... we were sitting, while looking towards 'Alee (ﷺ) as he was performing *Wudoo'*. He entered a handful of water into his mouth with his right hand and washed his mouth and nose and he then expelled the water from his nose with his left hand. He did this three times and then said, 'Whoever wants to see the way of purification of the Messenger of Allah (ﷺ), then this is his purification'.'

Shaykh Al-Albaanee said that this *Hadeeth* has an authentic chain of narrators in his notes on *Al-Mishkaat*. It is worth

5. Be thorough in rinsing the mouth and snuffing water, as mentioned in the <u>H</u>adeeth:

   ..and be thorough in snuffing water unless you are fasting.

   The meaning of being thorough in *rinsing the mouth* is to pass the water around to all parts of the mouth. The meaning of being thorough in *snuffing water* is to snuff the water to the uppermost part of the nose.

6. Rinse the mouth and place water of the nose for snuffing <u>with the same handful of water</u>:

   Then he (ﷺ) put his hand (in the water) and rinsed his mouth and snuffed up water (for cleaning the nose) from the palm of one hand...

   Note that the same handful of water was used — he (ﷺ) did not separate between the two action by using one handful for the first action and another for the second.

7. *Siwaak* and its position with regard to rinsing the mouth, from the <u>H</u>adeeth:

   Had it not been that I might cause hardship to my Ummah, I would have ordered them to use a Siwaak with every Wu<u>d</u>oo'?.

8. Run the fingers through a thick beard when washing the face.

---

noting that this follows the same principle mentioned in footnote 2 in the previous Chapter. Also, refer to the reference of *Zaad Al-Ma'aad* and by Ibn Al-Qayyim mentioned in <u>H</u>adeeth reference number 9 at the end of the booklet.

The Prophet (ﷺ) ran his fingers through his beard when performing Wudoo'.

9. Wipe the head.

The way of wiping the head is to start from the forehead until the nape of the neck and back to the front again.

As for what is obligatory of wiping the head, then it is wiping the whole of the head in any manner, from the front to the back and to the front again.

.. and the Messenger of Allah (ﷺ) wiped his head with his two hands from the front to the back and then to the front again... [14]

10. Run water through the fingers and toes:

Perform Wudoo' properly and run water through the fingers and toes. [15]

11. Begin with the right hand and foot:

The Prophet (ﷺ) preferred to begin with the right when wearing his sandals (shoes), combing his hair and in purification (Wudoo')... [16]

12. Increase washing from one to three times, when washing the face, arms and feet. [17]

13. Pronounce the *Shahaadah* upon completion:

«أَشْهَدُ أَنْ لَا إِلَهَ إِلَّا الله وَأَشْهَدُ أَنَّ مُحَمَّدًا عَبْدُهُ وَرَسُولُهُ»

I bear witness that there is no deity worthy of worship except Allah and I bear witness than Muhammad (ﷺ) is His Slave and Messenger.

The benefit of its pronunciation is that,

.. the eight doors of Paradise will be opened for him and he can enter from whichever one of them he desires.[18]

14. Perform *Wudoo'* at home:

Whoever purifies (i.e. performs Wudoo') in his house and then walk to one of the Houses of Allah (i.e. the Masjid) to perform an obligation of Allah (i.e. one of every two steps, a sin is removed and with the other, his level is raised (in Paradise).[19]

15. *Dalk* – this is to rub water over the body parts with the hand during *Wudoo'*.[20]

16. Economies in the use of water:

The Prophet (ﷺ) used to perform ablution with a Mudd[1] *of water.*[21]

17. Exceed the area of what is obligatory when washing the hands and feet:

When Aboo Hurayrah (ﷺ) performed his Wudoo', he washed his hand up to his upper arm (i.e. Up to his elbow and just beyond it) and then said, 'This is the way I saw the Messenger of Allah (ﷺ) perform Wudoo'...[22]

18. Perform two *Rak'ah* after completing *Wudoo'*:

Whoever performs Wudoo' in way that I perform it and then prays two Rak'ah of prayer and does not think of anything else (unrelated to the prayer) during it, his past sins will be forgiven.[23]

In another *Hadeeth* it was mentioned:

---

[1] See: Glossary of Terms, for an explanation of this word.

... Paradise would be made obligatory for him[24].

A muslim performs *Wudoo'* many times during the day and night. Some people perform it five times and others perform it more, depending on whether they pray additional optional prayers, such as *Salaah Ad-Duhaa* or *Qiyaam Al-Layl*.

Benefits of observing these *Sunan* in *Wudoo'*:

☐ The person will fall under the category of people in his (ﷺ) saying:

Whoever performs ablution well, the sins leave his body even from under his fingernails.[25]

☐ The Prophet (ﷺ) also said:

There is no one amongst you who performs Wudoo' well and then performs two Rak'ah of prayer with his heart and face (i.e. with Al-Khushoo;), except that Paradise will be made obligatory for him and he will be forgiven. [26]

General words of advice from Imaam An-Nawawee:

Indeed, a person obtains this level (of Al-Khushoo') by striving against his own self (i.e. his lowly desires) and against the whispering of Shaytaan – repulsing them from himself such that he is fully preoccupied with this striving, without losing focus even for the blink of an eye.

Hence, he is safeguarded from Shaytaan due to his striving and emptying his heart of everything that is harmful to it.

USING A *SIWAAK*

A *Siwaak* can be used on numerous occasions:

1. For every prayer, as the Prophet (ﷺ) said:

> Had it not been that I might cause hardship to my
> people, I would have ordered you to use a Siwaak for
> every prayer.[27]

The Muslim may use a *Siwaak* many times during the
night and day – for the five obligatory prayers, *Ar-
Rawaatib Sunnah*, prayers of *Ad-Duhaa*, *Al-Witr* etc.

2. When entering the house:

> When the Prophet (ﷺ) entered his home, he began by
> using a Siwaak.[28]

3. When reciting the Qur'an.

4. When the smell of the mouth changes.

5. When waking up.[29]

6. When performing *Wudoo'*:

> Siwaak is a purifier for the mouth and pleasing to the
> Lord.[30]

The benefits from implementing this *Sunnah*:

☐ The Pleasure of Allah (ﷺ) is on His slave,

☐ It is a purification of the mouth.

Modern medicine has discovered that *Siwaak* contains
many substances that are of benefit to humans,
especially for the gums. There are substances that
counteract germs, act as purifiers, have cleaning
properties for the teeth and freshen the smell and
taste of the mouth.

WEARING SHOES

Put shoes on starting with the right foot and take them off starting with the left:

When you put shoes on, begin with the right and when you remove them, begin with the left. Or, wear them both, or leave them both off [1] 31

The Muslim does this many times during the day and night–when entering and leaving the *Masjid*, the bathroom, the house, when going to work etc. Whenever the Muslim puts on or removes his shoes in accordance with the *Sunnah*, with this intention in mind, he obtains a great reward. And all his actions of *Harakaat* and *Sakanaat* will then be according to the *Sunnah*.

---

[1] i.e. do not wear just one shoe.

DRESSING AND UNDRESSING

1. Say *At-Tanmiyah* when dressing or undressing.

Imaam An-Nawawee said:

To say the Tasmiyah is preferred in all actions.[1]

2. Use the Prophet's (ﷺ) supplication.

When he put on a *Thawb*, long shirt, upper garment or turban, he would say:

«الْحَمْدُ للهِ الَّذِي كَسَانِي هَذَا (الثَّوبَ) وَرَزَقَنِيهِ مِنْ غَيْرِ حَوْلٍ مِنِّي وَلَا قُوَّةٍ. . »

All praise is for Allah, Who has clothed me with this garment and provided it for me, with no power or might from, myself.[2] 32

3. Begin with the right side:

When you wear clothes and perform *Wudoo'* begin with the right.33

4. Begin taking clothes off from the left side[3] .

---

[1] No evidence for saying the *Tasmiyah* when dressing was found. However, general evidences show the desirability of saying it before certain actions. The opinion of Imaam An-Nawawee is that is desirable to say it in all actions.

[2] The *Du'aa* found in the original Arabic manuscript has been replaced with this more authentic one.

[3] There is no specific evidence for this, but it seems that general evidences indicating to begin with the right (for things that are good) and the left for the opposite have been used. This was used in relation to putting on clothes, i.e. to put them on starting with the right; therefore, when taking them off, begin with the left.

ENTERING AND LEAVING THE HOUSE

Imaam An-Nawawee said it is preferable:

To say the Tasmiyah, increase in the remembrance of Allah and to greet the people.

1. Remember Allah when entering:

   When a man enters his house and mentions the Name of Allah while entering and while eating Shaytaan says (to the other Shayaateen), 'There is no abode for you and no food'.[34]

2. Supplicate when entering:

   «اللَّهُمَّ إِنِّي أَسْأَلُكَ خَيْرَ الْمَوْلَجِ وَخَيْرَ الْمَخْرَجِ بِسْمِ اللهِ وَلَجْنَا، وَبِسْمِ اللهِ خَرَجْنَا، وَعَلَى اللهِ رَبِّنَا تَوَكَّلْنَا» ثُمَّ لِيُسَلِّمْ عَلَى أَهْلِهِ

   O Allah, I ask You for the best of entering and the best of leaving. In the Name of Allah we enter, and in the Name of Allah we leave, and in our Lord, we place our trust.........and then to greet its inhabitants (i.e. family).[35]

   By this, the person is consciously seeking to put his reliance on Allah when entering and leaving the house. This is also a means to create a permanent bond with Allah.

3. Use a *Siwaak*:

   When the Prophet (ﷺ) entered his home, he began by using a Siwaak.[36]

4. Say the *Tasleem*:

$$\text{﴿فَإِذَا دَخَلْتُم بُيُوتًا فَسَلِّمُوا عَلَى أَنفُسِكُمْ تَحِيَّةً مِّنْ عِندِ اللَّهِ مُبَارَكَةً طَيِّبَةً﴾}$$

"... When you enter the houses, greet one another with a greeting from Allah, blessed and good..."

(*An-Noor*, 24:61)

'*Greeting from Allah*' means to say *Tasleem*.

5. Leave with the following supplication:

$$\text{«بِسْمِ اللهِ تَوَكَّلْتُ عَلَى اللهِ وَلَا حَوْلَ وَلَا قُوَّةَ إِلَّا بِاللهِ»}$$

In the Name of Allah, I place my trust in Allah, and there is no might or power except with Allah.

It will then be said to the one who says this:

$$\text{«كُفِيتَ وَوُقِيتَ وَتَنَحَّى عَنْهُ الشَّيْطَانُ»}$$

You have been sufficed and have been protected and Shaytaan has retreated.[37]

The Muslim enters and leaves his house many times during the day and nights: for prayer in the *Masjid*, work, household duties etc. If he practices these *Sunan* when he comes and goes, he will obtain for himself great benefit and reward.

Some benefits of practicing these *Sunan* are:

☐ The servant will be sufficed in his important affairs, whether worldly or religious matters.

☐ The servant will be protected from every evil and adversity, whether from *Jinn* or mankind.

☐ The servant will receive guidance – Allah will guide you in all of your religious and worldly affairs.

GOING TO THE *MASJID*

1. Go early, as the Prophet (ﷺ) said:

> *If mankind knew what (reward) was in the call[1] and in the first row[2] and found no other way to get that (reward) except by drawing lots, then they would have drawn lots.*

> *..... and if they knew what (reward) was in praying Salaah A*dh*-*Dh*uhr in its earliest time (Tahjeer) they would have raced for it....*

> *And if they knew the reward of Al-'Isha and Al-Fajr prayer in congregation, they would come to offer them even if they would come to offer them even if they had to crawl.*[38]

Imaam An-Nawawee said the word *Tahjeer* means to be early for the prayer.

2. Supplicate when going to the *Masjid*:

«اللَّهُمَّ اجْعَلْ فِي قَلْبِي نُورًا، وَفِي لِسَانِي نُورًا، وَاجْعَلْ فِي سَمْعِي نُورًا، وَاجْعَلْ فِي بَصَرِي نُورًا، وَاجْعَلْ مِنْ خَلْفِي نُورًا، وَمِنْ أَمَامِي نُورًا، وَاجْعَلْ مِنْ فَوْقِي نُورًا، وَمِنْ تَحْتِي نُورًا، اللَّهُمَّ أَعْطِنِي نُورًا»

O Allah, place light in my heart, and light on my tongue, and light within my ears, and light in my eyes, and place behind me light and in front of me light and above me light and beneath me light. O

---

[1] i.e. to pronounce the *Adhaan*.
[2] i.e. to pray in the first row of the congregational prayer.

Allah, bestow on me light![39]

3. Walk with *Sakeenah* and *Waqaar*.

If you hear the Iqaamah, then walk to the prayer with Sakeenah and Waqaar.[40]

- *Sakeenah* is to move calmly and avoid frivolity and

- *Waqaar is to lower the gaze and voice, and avoiding excessive looking around.*

4. Walk to the *Masjid*:

The jurists have stipulated that in order to increase the reward, it has been recommended in the *Sunnah* to go to the *Masjid* walking and to avoid haste. The *Sharee'ah* texts show the many merits in walking to the *Masjid*.

The Prophet ﷺ said:

'Shall I not show you something by which Allah removes your wrong-doings and raises your level (in Paradise)?'

'The (the Companions) said, 'Yes, O Messenger of Allah'. He (ﷺ) mentioned that from those things is taking many steps to the Masjid.[41]

5. Supplicate when entering the *Masjid*:

When one of you enters the Masjid, send Salaah on the Prophet (ﷺ) and say:

«اللَّهُمَّ افْتَحْ لِي أَبْوَابَ رَحْمَتِكَ»

O Allah, open for me the doors of your mercy. [42]

6. Enter with the right foot.

The saying of Anas bin Maalik (ﷺ):

From the Sunnah is that if you enter the Masjid, enter with your right foot and when you leave, leave with your left foot.[43]

7. Pray *Tahiyaat Al-Masjid* when entering:

When one of you enters the Masjid, do not sit until you pray two Rak'ah of prayer.[44]

Imaam Ash-Shaafi'ee said:

Tahiyaat Al-Masjid is legislated, even in the forbidden times.

Also, Imaam Al-Haafidh bin Hajar said:

The People of Fatwaa (i.e. the Scholars) agreed that Tahiyaat Al-Masjid is Sunnah.[1]

8. Proceed to the first row:

If mankind knew what (reward) was in the call[2] *and in the first row*[3] *and they found no other way to get that (reward) except by drawing lots, then they would have drawn lots.....*[45]

9. Supplicate when leaving the *Masjid*:

«اللَّهُمَّ إِنِّي أَسْأَلُكَ مِنْ فَضْلِكَ»

O Allah, I ask you from Your bounties.[46]

Also narrated by Aboo Daawood, with the addition of sending *Salaah* on the Prophet (ﷺ).

10. Leave with the left foot.[47]

---

[1] In this context, *Sunnah* is something that is not obligatory.

[2] i.e. to pronounce the *Adhaan*.

[3] i.e. to pray in the first row for the congregational prayer.

THE *ADHAAN*

There are five *Sunan* of the *Adhaan* as mentioned by
Ibn Al-Qayyim in *Zaad Al-Ma'aad* :

1. The Person hearing the *Adhaan* repeats what the
   Mu'adhadhin says, except for when he hears:

$$\text{«حَيَّ عَلَى الصَّلَاةِ، حَيَّ عَلَى الْفَلَاحِ»}$$

Come to prayer. Com to prosperity
... instead, he says:

$$\text{«لَا حَوْلَ وَلَا قُوَّةَ إِلَّا بِاللهِ»}$$

There is no might, or power, except with Allah.[48]

The benefit of this *Sunnah* is that it makes Paradise
obligatory, as mentioned in the narration by *Muslim*.

2. Then, the one hearing the *Adhaan* should say:

$$\text{«وَأَنَا أَشْهَدُ أَنْ لَا إِلَهَ إِلَّا اللهُ وَحْدَهُ لَا شَرِيكَ لَهُ وَأَنَّ مُحَمَّدًا}$$
$$\text{عَبْدُهُ وَرَسُولُهُ، رَضِيتُ بِاللهِ رَبًّا وَبِمُحَمَّدٍ رَسُولًا وَبِالْإِسْلام دِينًا»}$$

*And I also bear witness that there is no deity worthy
of worship except Allah, alone without any partners,
and I bear witness that Muhammad (ﷺ) is His Slave
and Messenger. I am pleased with Allah as the Lord,
with Muhammad as the Messenger and with Islam as
the religion.*[49]

The benefit of this Sunnah is that the person's sins
would be forgiven.

3. Then, send *Salaah* on the Prophet (ﷺ):

*When you hear the Mu'adhdhin, say as he says, then
send Salaah on me for whoever sends Salah on me,
Allah sends Salaah on him ten times.*[50]

The fullest form is *Salaah Al-Ibraaheemiyyah* :

«اللَّهُمَّ صَلِّ عَلَى مُحَمَّدٍ وَعَلَى آلِ مُحَمَّدٍ، كَمَا صَلَّيْتَ عَلَى
إِبْرَاهِيمَ وَعَلَى آلِ إِبْرَاهِيمَ، إِنَّكَ حَمِيدٌ مَجِيدٌ، اللَّهُمَّ بَارِكْ عَلَى
مُحَمَّدٍ وَعَلَى آلِ مُحَمَّدٍ كَمَا بَارَكْتَ عَلَى إِبْرَاهِيمَ وَعَلَى آلِ
إِبْرَاهِيمَ، إِنَّكَ حَمِيدٌ مَجِيدٌ»

*O Allah, send Salaah on Muhammad and his family,
as you sent Salaah on Ibraaheem and his family.
Verily you are Praised, Majestic.*

*O Allah, send blessings on Muhammad and his family
as you sent blessings on Ibraaheem and his family.
Verily you are Praised, Majestic.*[51]

The meaning of Allah's *Salaah* on his servant is Allah
praising the servant in the highest of gatherings (i.e.
of the angels).

4. After the *Salaah* on the Prophet (ﷺ), say:

«اللَّهُمَّ رَبَّ هَذِهِ الدَّعْوَةِ التَّامَّةِ، وَالصَّلَاةِ الْقَائِمَةِ، آتِ مُحَمَّدًا
الْوَسِيلَةَ وَالْفَضِيلَةَ، وَابْعَثْهُ مَقَامًا مَحْمُودًا الَّذِي وَعَدْتَهُ»

*O Allah, Lord of this Perfect Call and Owner of this
Prayer to be performed, bestow on Muhammad Al-
Waseelah and Al-Fadeelah that You promised him.*[52]

The benefit of this supplication is that whoever says
it will be granted the Prophet's (ﷺ) intercession on
the Day of Resurrection.

5. Finally, supplicate for oneself, asking Allah from His Bounty; for surely He will respond:

Say as they are saying (i.e. the Mu'adhdhin). When you have finished, ask (supplicate), for it will be given to you.[53]

THE *IQAAMAH*

Perform points 1 to 4 as mentioned in the previous Chapter – *Sunan of the Adhaan*.[54]

Just as for the *Adhaan*, the *Sunnah* for the one hearing the *Iqaamah* is to repeat what the person calling the *Iqaamah* say. However, when he says,

«حَيَّ عَلَى الصَّلَاةِ، حَيَّ عَلَى الْفَلَاحِ»

Come to prayer, come to prosperity.

..... one should not repeat this, but instead say:

«لَا حَوْلَ وَلَا قُوَّةَ إِلَّا بِالله»

There is no might, or power, except with Allah.

Note, when the person calling the *Iqaamah says*,

«قَدْ قَامَتِ الصَّلَاةُ»

The Salaah is about to be established.

.. the person hearing it should say likewise and he should <u>not</u> say,

«أَقَامَهَا اللهُ وَأَدَامَهَا»

Allah has established it (the prayer) and has preserved.

.. as the <u>H</u>adeeth that mentions this week.[55]

PRAYING TOWARDS A *SUTRAH*

The Prophet ﷺ said:

> *When one of you prays, pray towards a Sutrah. Stand close to it and do not let anyone pass between you and it.* [56]

This text is general regarding taking a *Sutrah* – irrespective of whether it is in the *Masjid* or home, for men or women. Some people do not adopt this *Sunnah*, so we find them praying without a *Sutrah*. This *Sunnah* is repeated by a Muslim many times during the day and night-for the *Sunnah Ar-Rawaatib*, *Ad-Duhaa*, *Tahiyaat Al-Masjid* and *Al-Witr* prayers. For a woman it is repeated when she prays her obligatory prayers at home. As for the congregational prayers, the Imaam is the *Sutrah* for those behind him.

ISSUES REGARDING THE *SUTRAH*

1. The *Sutrah* can be whatever the person praying sets in from of him when he is facing the *Qiblah* – such as a wall, stick or pillar. There is no limit to its width.

2. It should be at least the height of the back of a saddle (about a hand span). [57]

3. The space from the feet to the *Sutrah* should be about three arm-spans so that there is sufficient room for *Sajdah*.

4. The *Sutrah* has been legislated for the *Imaam* as well as for the person praying alone, for the obligatory and options prayers alike. [59]

5. The *Sutrah* of the *Imaam* is the *Sutrah* of the people

praying behind him. It is permissible to walk between the lines of the people praying (i.e. in front of them), if there is a need.[60]

Benefits of observing this *Sunnah*:

☐ It protects the prayer from being broken.

☐ When someone passes in from of a praying person, it cuts or reduces the value of the prayer. Things that break the *Salaah*, when they pass between the one praying and his *Sutrah*, are a female past the age of puberty, and a black dog.[61]

☐ The person praying provides a apace for the people to pass by, thereby not giving them a need to pass directly in front of him.

☐ It protects the eyes from wandering and looking around, because the person using the *Sutrah* would always focus his sight to the area before his *Sutrah*. In this way, it is easier to contemplate on the meanings of the prayer.

THE OPTIONAL PRAYERS

1. *Ar- Rawaatib* prayers:

There is not a Muslim servant who prays to Allah twelve Rak'aat, other than the obligatory prayers, every day and in obedience to Him, except that Allah builds for him a house in Paradise; or a house will be built for him in Paradise.[62]

These extra, recommended prayers are:

• Four *Rak'aat* before *Salaah Adh-Dhuhr* and two after it.

• Two *Rak'ah* after *Salaah Al-Maghrib,*

• Two *Rak'aah* after *Salaah Al-'Isha* and

• Two *Rak'aah* before *Salaah Al-Fajr.*

My dear brother, do you not yearn for a house in Paradise?

Preserve this Prophetic advice and perform twelve *Rak'aah,* in addition to the obligation prayers.

2. *Salaah Ad-Duhaa*.

In the human dody, there are three hundred and sixty joints. In order to express gratitude for this blessing, charity is required to be given on behalf of every one of these joints daily; yet, the full reward of this, can be attained by praying the two *Rak'ah* of *Ad-Duhaa*:

Every morning, charity is due on every joint of a person – every Tasbeeh is a charity, to enjoin good is a charity and to forbid evil is a charity. All of this is sufficed by two Rak'ah prayed at Ad-Duhaa.[63]

Aboo Hurayrah (ﷺ) said:

My friend (ﷺ) advised me to fast three days of every month[1] *... pray two Rak'ah of Ad-Duhaa and pray Al-Witr before lying down (to sleep)....*[64]

Its time begins approximately fifteen minutes after the sun rises and lasts until approximately fifteen minutes before *Salaah Adh-Dhuhr*. The best or preferred time to perform it is at the time of preferred time to perform it is at the time of intense heat. The minimum number of *Rak'aat* is two and the maximum is eight. It has also been said that there is no limit to the number.

3. *Sunnah* of *Salaah Al-'Asr*:

May Allah have mercy on a person who prays four Rak'aat before Salaah Al-Asr.[65]

4. *Sunnah of Salaah Al-Maghrib*:

'Pray before the obligatory prayer of Maghrib'. 'He said it three times and on the third time he said, 'For whoever wants'.[66]

5. *Sunnah of Salaah Al-'Isha*:

'Between (every) two calls to prayer is a prayer. 'Between (every) two calls to prayer is a prayer. 'Between (every) two calls to prayer is a prayer.' On the third time he added, 'For whoever wants'.[67]

Imaam An-Nawawee said the intended meaning of *'the two calls to prayer'* is the *Adhaan* and *Iqaamah*.

---

[1] i.e. the three day of the full moon, which are the 13th — 15th of the lunar month.

THE NIGHT PRAYER

Regarding *Qiyaam Al-Layl*, the Prophet(ﷺ) said:

The most excellent fast after the month of Ramadan, is fasting in the month of Allah, 'Al-Muharram'. And the most excellent prayer after the obligatory prayer is the night prayer.[68]

1. The preferred number of *Rak'aat* for the night prayer is eleven or thirteen, with prolonged standing:

   The Prophet (ﷺ) prayed eleven Rak'aat and that was his prayer....[69]

   In another narration,

   He (ﷺ) prayed, in the night, thirteen Rak'aat...[70]

2. It is recommended that when a person gets up for *Qiyaam Al-Layl*, he cleans his teeth with a *Siwaak*[71] and recites the last Verses of *Soorah Aal-'Imraan*, from:

   ﴿إِنَّ فِى خَلْقِ ٱلسَّمَٰوَٰتِ وَٱلْأَرْضِ وَٱخْتِلَٰفِ ٱلَّيْلِ وَٱلنَّهَارِ لَءَايَٰتٍ لِّأُوْلِى ٱلْأَلْبَٰبِ﴾

   "Verily, in the creation of the heavens and the earth, and in the alternation of night and day there are indeed signs for men of understanding."

   (Aal-'Imraan, 3:190)

   ......until the end of the *Soorah*.[72]

3. It is recommended to supplicate, using this authentic

Du'aa of the Prophet (ﷺ).[1]

«اللَّهُمَّ لَكَ الْحَمْدُ أَنْتَ قَيِّمُ السَّمْوَاتِ وَالأَرْضِ وَمَنْ فِيهِنَّ
وَلَكَ الْحَمْدُ، أَنْتَ نُورُ السَّمْوَاتِ وَالأَرْضِ وَمَنْ فِيهِنَّ، وَلَكَ
الْحَمْدُ، لَكَ مُلْكُ السَّمْوَاتِ وَالأَرْضِ وَمَنْ فِيهِنَّ وَلَكَ
الْحَمْدُ، أَنْتَ مَلِكُ السَّمْوَاتِ وَالأَرْضِ وَلَكَ الْحَمْدُ، أَنْتَ
الْحَقُّ، وَوَعْدُكَ الْحَقُّ، وَلِقَاؤُكَ حَقٌّ، وَقَوْلُكَ حَقٌّ، وَالْجَنَّةُ
حَقٌّ، وَالنَّارُ حَقٌّ، وَالنَّبِيُّونَ حَقٌّ، وَمُحَمَّدٌ حَقٌّ، وَالسَّاعَةُ حَقٌّ
اللَّهُمَّ لَكَ أَسْلَمْتُ، وَبِكَ آمَنْتُ، وَعَلَيْكَ تَوَكَّلْتُ، وَإِلَيْكَ
أَنَبْتُ، وَبِكَ خَاصَمْتُ، وَإِلَيْكَ حَاكَمْتُ، فَاغْفِرْ لِي مَا
قَدَّمْتُ، وَمَا أَخَّرْتُ، وَمَا أَسْرَرْتُ، وَمَا أَعْلَنْتُ أَنْتَ الْمُقَدِّمُ،
وَأَنْتَ الْمُؤَخِّرُ لَا إِلَهَ إِلَّا أَنْتَ (أَوْ لَا إِلَهَ غَيْرُكَ)»

*O Allah, for You is all praise. You are the custodian of
the heavens and the earth and whatever is in them and
for You is all praise.*

*You are the Source of Light of the heavens and the
earth and whatever is in them and for You is all
praise.*

*Yours is the dominion of the heavens and the earth
and whatever is in them and for You is all praise.*

*You are King of the heavens and earth and for You is
all praise.*

You are Truth and Your promise is the truth and the

---

[1] When waking up for the night prayer, the Prophet (ﷺ) used
to read this *Du'aa*, <u>after making *Takbeer*</u>, as narrated in
another *Hadeeth* by Al-Bukhaaree.

meeting with You is true and Your Word is true and Paradise is true and the Fire is true and the Prophets are true and Muhammad ﷺ is true and the Hour is true.

O Allah, to You I have submitted and in You I have believed and on You I have placed my trust and to You I have repented and over You I have disputed and to You I have turned for judgement.

So, forgive me for my sins that have turned for judgment.

So, forgive me for my sins that have come to pass and of my sins that will come to pass and what I have concealed and what I have made public.

You are Al-Muqaddim and Al-Mu'akhkhir. There is no deity worthy of worship except You (or there is no deity worthy of worship other than You).[73]

4. Also from the *Sunnah of Qiyaam Al-Layl*, is to begin with two short *Rak'ah*, so that you become active for what comes after:

When one of you stands up for the night prayer, begin with two light Rak'ah (i.e. short).[74]

5. It is recommend to begin with the authentic supplication established from the Prophet (ﷺ):

«اللَّهُمَّ رَبَّ جِبْرَائِيلَ، وَمِيكَائِيلَ، وَإِسْرَافِيلَ فَاطِرَ السَّمْوَاتِ وَالْأَرْضِ، عَالِمَ الْغَيْبِ وَالشَّهَادَةِ، أَنْتَ تَحْكُمُ بَيْنَ عِبَادِكَ فِيمَا كَانُوا فِيهِ يَخْتَلِفُونَ. اهْدِنِي لِمَا اخْتُلِفَ فِيهِ مِنَ الْحَقِّ بِإِذْنِكَ إِنَّكَ تَهْدِي مَنْ تَشَاءُ إِلَى صِرَاطٍ مُسْتَقِيمٍ»

O Allah, the Lord of Jibraa'eel, Meekaa'eel and

Israafeel, Originator of the heavens and the earth, Knower of the seen and unseen.

You are the One Who arbitrates between Your servants in that which they dispute. Guide me to the truth by Your leave in that which they have differed. Verily, You guide whomsoever You will to the straight path.[75]

6. It is recommended to lengthen the prayer:

The Messenger of Allah (ﷺ) was asked, 'which prayer is the most excellent prayer?' He said, 'That prayer in which there is prolonged Qunoot'.[76]

The meaning of *Qunoot*[1] here is *Qiyaam* – the standing position in prayer.

7. It is recommended to:

• Seek refuge in Allah on hearing or reading Verses of punishment by saying,

«أَعُوذُ بِاللهِ مِنَ عَذَابِ اللهِ»

I seek refuge in Allah from Allah's Punishment.

• Ask for His Mercy on Verses of mercy,

« اللَّهُمَّ إِنِّي أَسْأَلُكَ مِنْ فَضْلِكَ»

O Allah, I ask You from Your bounties.

• Praise Him on Verses of glorification,

---

[1] Refer to the explanation of this *Hadeeth* in *Saheeh Muslim* by Imaam An-Nawawee, in which it is mentioned that the meaning of *Qunoot*, in the *Hadeeth*, is *Qiyaam*.

«سُبْحَانَ اللهِ»

Far removed is Allah from any imperfection.
This is from the <u>H</u>adeeth :

...he (ﷺ) read slowly (with reflection). If he read a Verse of glorification, he glorified Him. If he read a Verse of request, he asked from Him. If he read a Verse seeking refuge, he sought refuge in Him[1] ....

Things that help one to perform *Qiyaam Al-Layl* :

○ Supplication.[2]

○ Avoid staying up late at night.

○ Rest between A<u>dh-Dh</u>uhr *and* A<u>s</u>r *(Qayloolah)*.

○ Refrain from all forms of disobedience.

○ Strive against one's desires.

---

[1] This <u>H</u>adeeth states that the Prophet (ﷺ) glorified Allah, requested Him and sought refuge in Him. However, no specific wording for how he (ﷺ) did this was mentioned. Therefore, the *Shaykh* has given us some examples of what can be said.

[2] i.e. ask Allah to assist you and make it easy for you.

THE *WITR* PRAYER

1. Whoever performs three *Rak'aat* of *Al-Witr*, should read the following after *Al-Faatihah* :[78]

In the first *Rak'ah*,

$$ ﴿سَبِّحِ اسْمَ رَبِّكَ الْأَعْلَى﴾ $$

"Glorify the Name of you Lord, most High..."
(Al-A'laa, 87 : 1 -19)

In the second,

$$ ﴿قُلْ يَا أَيُّهَا الْكَافِرُونَ﴾ $$

"Say: 'O you disbelievers...'"
(Al-Kaafiroon, 109 : 1 - 6)

And in third,

$$ ﴿قُلْ هُوَ اللَّهُ﴾ $$

"Say : 'He is Allah the One, the Unique...'"
(Al-Ikhlaas, 112 : 1 - 4)

2. Say after *Tasleem* (at the end of the prayer):

$$ «سُبْحَانَ الْمَلِكِ الْقُدُّوسِ» . $$

Far removed is the King, the Holy from any imperfections. (Three times)[79]

And in another narration, collected by Ad-Daaraqutni,

After the final saying of,

«سُبْحَانَ الْمَلِكِ الْقُدُّوسِ» .

...he (ﷺ) raised and prolonged his voice and said,

«رَبُّ الْمَلَائِكَةِ وَالرُّوحِ» .

*The Lord of the angels and Ar-Roo*h.[1]

---

[1] In this context, *Ar-Roo*h refers to the angel Jibraa'eel.

THE *FAJR* PRAYER

<u>S</u>alaah Al-Fajr has specific *Sunan* related to it, from among them is to :

1. Shorten the length of *Sunnah* prayer, on the authority of 'Aishah (ﷺ):

   The Prophet (ﷺ) prayed two short Rak'ah between the Adhaan and Iqaamah of Fajr prayer.[80]

2. From the recommended Verses to recite in the *Sunnah* prayer, are the following:[81]

In the first *Rak'ah*,

$$﴿ \ldots \text{ قُولُوٓا۟ ءَامَنَّا بِٱللَّهِ وَمَآ أُنزِلَ إِلَيۡنَا} ﴾$$

"*Say: 'We believe in Allah and what was sent down to us...'*"

(Al-Baqarah, 2 :136)

And in the last *Rak'ah* either read,

$$﴿ ءَامَنَّا بِٱللَّهِ وَٱشۡهَدۡ بِأَنَّا مُسۡلِمُونَ ﴾$$

"*We believe in Allah and bear witness that we are Muslims.*"

(Aal-'Imraan, 3 : 52)

... or read,

$$﴿ قُلۡ يَٰٓأَهۡلَ ٱلۡكِتَٰبِ تَعَالَوۡا۟ إِلَىٰ كَلِمَةٍ سَوَآءِۭ بَيۡنَنَا وَبَيۡنَكُمۡ \ldots ﴾$$

"*Say : 'O people of the Scripture, come to a word that is just between us and you...'*"

(Aal-'Imraan, 3 :64)

Alternatively, read in the *first Rak'ah* :,[82]

﴿قُلْ يَٰٓأَيُّهَا ٱلْكَٰفِرُونَ﴾

"*Say : 'O you disbelievers...'*"

(*Al-Kaafiroon, 109 : 1 -6*)

And in the *last Rak'ah,*

﴿قُلْ هُوَ ٱللَّهُ﴾

"*Say : 'He is Allah, the One and Unique...'*"

(*Al-Ikhlaas,112 : 1 - 4*)

3. Take a rest after the *Sunnah* prayer:

When the Prophet (ﷺ) prayed two Rak'ah of the Sunnah prayer of Al-Fajr, he would lie down on his right side.[1]

After you have prayed the two *Rak'ah* of the *Sunnah* of *Al-Fajr,* try to lie down on your right side, even for a minute or so, so that you can fulfill this *Sunnah.*

---

[1] The general practice of the Prophet (ﷺ) was to pray the *Sunnah* of *Al-Fajr* at home.

SITTING AFTER THE *FAJR* PRAYER

It is from the *Sunnah to sit after the prayer*:

When the Prophet (ﷺ) prayed Al-Fajr, he sat in his place until the sun rose <u>Hassanaa</u>. [84]

Imaam An-Nawawee said <u>Hassanaa</u>, in this grammatical form, means 'risen perfectly'. [1]

Benefit of sitting in the *Masjid*:

Allah (ﷻ) instructed the angels to pray for forgiveness for those sitting in the Masaajid, whether it is before or after the <u>S</u>alaah, by saying:

«اللَّهُمَّ اغْفِرْ لَهُ»

O Allah, forgive him.

«اللَّهُمَّ ارْحَمْهُ»

O Allah, have Mercy on him. [85]

What is a greater blessing than this? Look at your status with Allah if you obey Him. The angels – the creation that is close to Allah – are instructed to supplicate for you!

---

[1] i.e. has completely cleared the horizon.

WHAT IS SAID DURING THE PRAYER

From the *Sunan of what should be said during the prayer*, is:

1. Recite the opening supplication after the first *Takbeer* (*Takbeer Al-Iḥraam*):

«سُبْحَانَكَ اللَّهُمَّ وَبِحَمْدِكَ، وَتَبَارَكَ اسْمُكَ، وَتَعَالَى جَدُّكَ، وَلَا إِلَهَ غَيْرُكَ»

Far removed are you from any imperfection, O Allah and praise be to You.

Blessed be your Name and lofty is Your position.

And none has the right to be worshipped except You.
[86]

Alternatively, you may say:

«اللَّهُمَّ بَاعِدْ بَيْنِي وَبَيْنَ خَطَايَايَ كَمَا بَاعَدْتَ بَيْنَ الْمَشْرِقِ وَالْمَغْرِبِ، اللَّهُمَّ نَقِّنِي مِنَ الْخَطَايَا، كَمَا يُنَقَّى الثَّوْبُ الْأَبْيَضُ مِنَ الدَّنَسِ، اللَّهُمَّ اغْسِلْ خَطَايَايَ بِالْمَاءِ وَالثَّلْجِ وَالْبَرَدِ»

O Allah, distance me from my sins just You have distanced the east from the west. O Allah, purify me of my sins as a white Thawb is purified of filth. O Allah, cleanse me of my sins with snow, water and ice.[87]

2. Seek refuge in Allah before reciting from the Qur'an:

أَعُوذُ بِاللهِ مِنَ الشَّيْطَانِ الرَّجِيمِ

I seek refuge in Allah from Shaytaan, the accursed.[88]

3. Then recite *Al-Basmala* :

In the Name of Allah – the most Gracious, the most Merciful.[89]

4. Say آمِين (*Ameen*) after reciting *Al-Faatihah*.[90]

5. Recite a *Soorah* after *Al-Faatihah*.

The person praying alone should recite a *Soorah*, or part of one, after *Al-Faatihah* in the first two *Rak'ah* of all prayers.

For the one who is praying behind the *Imaam* in congregation, he should read a *Soorah* after *Al-Faatihah* in the first two *Rak'ah* of the <u>silent</u> prayers.

As for the first two *Rak'ah* of the <u>loud</u> prayers, he does not read but instead listens to the *Imaam's* recitation.[91]

6. Supplicate upon rising from *Rukoo'* :

«رَبَّنَا لَكَ الْحَمْد»

Our Lord, to You be all praise.[92]

And then say:

«مِلْءُ السَّمَوَاتِ وَمِلْءُ الأَرْضِ وَمِلْءُ مَا شِئْتَ مِنْ شَيْءٍ بَعْدُ، أَهْلَ الثَّنَاءِ وَالْمَجْدِ أَحَقُّ مَا قَالَ الْعَبْدُ وَكُلُّنَا لَكَ عَبْدٌاللَّهُمَّ لَا مَانِعَ لِمَا أَعْطَيْتَ وَلَا مُعْطِيَ لِمَا مَنَعْتَ وَلَا يَنْفَعُ ذَا الْجَدِّ مِنْكَ الْجَدُّ»

The heavens and the earth and all that is between them

abound with Your praises and all that You will abound with Your praises.

O Possessor of praise and majesty, the truest thing a slave had said (of You) and we are all Your slaves.

O Allah, none can prevent what You willed to bestow and none can bestow what you willed to prevent and no wealth or majesty can benefit anyone, as all Wealth and Majesty is from You.[93]

7. Repeat the *Tasbeeh* more than once:[94]

The *Tasbeeh* while <u>bowing</u>:

$$ «سُبْحَانَ رَبِّيَ الْعَظِيمِ» $$

Far removed is my Lord from any imperfections, the Supreme.

The *Tasbeeh* while <u>prostrating</u>:

$$ «سُبْحَانَ رَبِّيَ الأَعْلَى» $$

Far removed is my Lord from any imperfections, the Most High.

8. Repeat this supplication more than once while sitting between the two prostrations:

$$ «رَبِّ اغْفِرْ لِي» $$

My Lord, forgive me.[95]

9. Supplicate after the final *Tashshahud*:

$$ «اللَّهُمَّ إِنِّي أَعُوذُ بِكَ مِنْ عَذَابِ جَهَنَّمَ وَمِنْ عَذَابِ الْقَبْرِ وَمِنْ فِتْنَةِ الْمَحْيَا وَالْمَمَاتِ وَمِنْ شَرِّ فِتْنَةِ الْمَسِيحِ الدَّجَّالِ» $$

O Allah, verily I seek refuge with You from the punishment of Hell and the punishment of the grave and from the trials of life and death and from the evil trial of the Dajjaal.[96]

10. Lengthen the supplication when prostrating.

It is preferred for the person not to shorten the supplication after the initial *Tasbeeh* in prostration but on the contrary to increase the supplication, as he wills. This is taken from the following *Hadeeth*:

The closest the servant is to his Lord, is when he is prostrating – so increase the supplication in it.[97]

Points to note:

☐ The *Sunan* of speech are performed in every *Rak'ah*, except the opening supplication and the supplication after the *Tashshahud*.

☐ There are other supplications. Whoever desires to know then may refer to *Hisn Al-Muslim* by Shaykh Sa'eed Al-Qahtaanee.

So, the total number of the *Sunan* mentioned above, in the obligatory prayers, amounts to ten. As for the optional prayers performed in the day and night in which these two *Sunan* are repeated, their total amounts to twenty-four *Sunan*. This may be increased by performing *Qiyaam Al-Layl*, *Ad-Duhaa* and *Tahiyaat Al-Masjid*. By performing more often the *Sunan* that occur once in the *Salaah*, the person's reward will be increased and his hold on the *Sunnah* strengthened.

ACTIONS PERFORMED
IN THE PRAYER

From the *Sunan* actions of the prayer, is:

1. Raise the hands at the following times:

- When saying *Takbeer Al-Ihraam*.[98]

- When going into *Rukoo'*.[99]

- When rising from *Rukoo'*.[100]

- When standing up for the third *Rak'ah*.[101]

2. The manner of raising the hands:

- When raising and lowering the hands, the fingers should be close together, stretched out and with the palms of the hands facing the *Qiblah*.[102]

- Raise the hands – either to the side of the shoulders or to the bottom of the ears.[103]

3. Place the right hand on the left, or grasp the left wrist bone with your right hand.[104]

4. Look towards the place of prostration.[105]

5. Separate your feet to a comfortable distance when standing.

6. Recite the Qur'aan with *Tarteel* and contemplate on what is being said:[106]

"And recite the Qur'aan (aloud) with Tarteel."
         (Al-Muzzammil, 73 :4)

AR-RUKOO'

From the *Sunan* of *Rukoo'*, is:

1. Grasp the knees with the hands, while the fingers are apart.[107]

2. Extend the back so that it is flat.[108]

3. The head should be in line with the back, without lowering it or raising it.[1] [109]

4. Keep the upper arms away from the side of the body.[110]

---

[1] i.e. the head should be in line with the straightened back.

AS-SUJOOD

From the *Sunan* of *Sujood*, is:

1. To keep the upper arms away from the side of the body.[111]

2. To keep the stomach away from the thighs.

3. To ensure the thighs are away from the shins.[1]

4. To separate the knees.[2]

5. To keep the feet upright.[112]

6. To ensure the toes face the *Qiblah*, so that the joints of the toes rest on the floor.[113]

7. To press the feet together for the duration of the prostration.[114]

8. To place the hands in line with the shoulders or ears.[115]

9. To straighten the hands.[116]

10. To ensure the fingers are close together.[117]

11. To ensure the fingers are pointing towards the *Qiblah*.[118]

---

[1] i.e. keep the hamstrings away from the calves.

[2] No specific evidence was found for Points 2 to 4. However, from the description of the Prophet's (ﷺ) *Sajdah*, he (ﷺ) was not cramped up, but rather he was spread out.

AL-JALSAH

1. The sitting (or *Jalsah*) <u>between</u> the prostration is of two types:

• The first is called *Al-Iqaa'*, which it is to sit on the heels with both feet upright.[1] 199

• The second is called *Al-Iftiraash*. This is to keep the right foot in an upright position and lay the <u>left foot flat on the floor.</u>

2. The sitting for the first *Tashshahud* is also *Al-Iftiraash*, except that it is <u>to sit on the left foot</u> with the right foot upright.120

It is *Sunnah* to lengthen *Jalash Al-Iftiraash* :

The Prophet (ﷺ) used to lengthen this sitting, until a person would say, 'Perhaps, he has forgotten (to continue)'.[2] 121

3. The other type of sitting is called *Jalsah Al-Istiraahah*.[3] It is performed after the second prostration before standing up, in the first and third *Rak'ah*. There are no supplications in it and the *Sunnah* is to sit briefly.122

---

[1] This type of sitting is only permitted for the sitting between the two prostrations and not for the *Tashshahud*.

[2] This is an indication that the Prophet (ﷺ) used to sit in this position for a long time.

[3] *Jalash Al-Istiraahah* is performed in the same manner as *Jalash Al-Iftiraash* is performed for the first *Tashshahud*.

THE FINAL *TASHAHHUD*

1. This final sitting has three forms:

- *At-Tawarruk :* This is to keep the right foot upright, while placing the left foot under the right shin and to sit on the floor.[123]

- Sit in the same position as above, except that the right foot is not placed upright, but it follows the direction of the left[124]

- To keep the right foot upright and to place the left leg between the shin and thigh of right leg.[125]

2. Place the hands on the thighs – the right hand on the right thigh and the left hand on the left thigh – with the fingers outstretched and close together.[126]

3. Point with the index finger, during this *Tashahhud,* from the beginning to the end and connect the thumb with the middle finger to form a circle. Focus the sight on the index finger.[127]

4. *At-Tasleem :* This is to turn the head to the right then left when finishing the prayer.[128]

Summary of actions in the prayer:

There are twenty-five *Sunan* pertaining to the actions repeated in every *Rak'ah*. From amongst those *Sunan* that are not repeated in the prayer more than once or twice:

☐ To raise the hands with initial *Takbeer*.

☐ To raise the hands to the shoulders or bottom of the ears when standing up for the third *Rak'ah*, in prayer comprising of two *Tashahhuds*.

☐ To point with the index finger from the beginning of the *Tashshahud* to the end of it, whether it is the first or second *Tashahhud*.

☐ *Jalsah Al-Istiraahah*, which is repeated twice, in the prayer consisting of four *Rak'aat*, and once in the remaining prayers, whether it is an obligatory or voluntary prayer.

☐ *At-Tawarruk*: This is in the second *Tashahhud*, in a prayer with two *Tashahhuds*.

☐ To turn the head to the right and the left in concluding the prayer *(Tasleem)*.

These *Sunan* are all repeated once, except the pointing with the index finger during *Tashshahud* which is performed twice in every obligatory prayer (apart from *Salaah Al-Fajr*) and *Jalsah Al-Istiraahah*, which is repeated twice in a four-*Rak'aat* prayer. These *Sunan* total thirty-four.

Strive to beautify your prayer by implementing these *Sunan* of speech and action so that your reward is increased and your status with Allah is raised.

General words of advice from Ibn Al-Qayyim:

The servant is between the Hands of Allah in two situations. The first is during the time of prayer and the second is on the Day of Meeting (i.e. the Day of Judgment).

So, whoever fulfils his duty in the first situation will have ease in the second, and whoever underestimates the importance of the first situation and does not fulfill its rights, will have hardships in the second.

AFTER THE OBLIGATORY PRAYERS

There are many *Adhkaar* that can be said after the obligatory prayer. From among them is:

1. To say:

أَسْتَغْفِرُ اللهَ (ثلاث مرات)

I seek the forgiveness of Allah. (Three times)

Followed by,

اللَّهُمَّ أَنْتَ السَّلَامُ وَمِنْكَ السَّلَامُ

تَبَارَكْتَ يَا ذَا الْجَلَالِ وَالإِكْرَامِ

O Allah, You are Peace and from You is all Peace.

Blessed are You, O Possessor of Majesty and Honour.[129]

2. To say:

سُبْحَانَ اللهِ (ثلاثاً وثلاثين مَرةً)

Far removed is Allah from any imperfections. (Thirty-three times)

الْحَمْدُ للهِ (ثلاثاً وثلاثين مَرةً)

All praise is for Allah. (Thiry-times)

اللهُ أَكْبَرُ (ثلاثاً وثلاثين مَرةً)

Allah is the Greatest. (Thirty-three times)

On completion of this, then say:

«لَا إِلَهَ إِلَّا اللهُ وَحْدَهُ لَا شَرِيكَ لَهُ لَهُ الْمُلْكُ وَلَهُ الْحَمْدُ وَهُوَ
عَلَى كُلِّ شَيْءٍ قَدِيرٌ»

*There is no deity worthy of worship, except Allah alone,
having no partners. To Him belongs all sovereignty and
praise and He is over all things, Ominipotent.*[130]

3. To say:

«لَا إِلَهَ إِلَّا اللهُ وَحْدَهُ لَا شَرِيكَ لَهُ لَهُ الْمُلْكُ وَلَهُ الْحَمْدُ يُحْيِي
وَيُمِيتُ وَهُوَ عَلَى كُلِّ شَيْءٍ قَدِيرٌ» (عَشَرَ مَرَّاتٍ)

*There is no deity worthy of worship, except Allah alone,
having no partners. To Him belongs all sovereignty and
praise. He gives life and death and He is over all things,
Omnipotent.*

To be said ten times after the *Maghrib* and *Fajr*
prayers. [131]

All of these praises should be counted on the hand.
There is a difference of opinion about the authenticity
of narration specifying the use of only the right hand,
but there are general evidences that indicate the use of
the right hand.[132]

4. To say:

«لَا إِلَهَ إِلَّا اللهُ وَحْدَهُ لَا شَرِيكَ لَهُ لَهُ الْمُلْكُ وَلَهُ الْحَمْدُ وَهُوَ
عَلَى كُلِّ شَيْءٍ قَدِيرٌ. اللَّهُمَّ لَا مَانِعَ لِمَا أَعْطَيْتَ وَلَا مُعْطِيَ لِمَا
مَنَعْتَ وَلَا يَنْفَعُ ذَا الْجَدِّ مِنْكَ الْجَدُّ»

*There is no deity worthy of worship, except Allah alone,
having no partners. To Him belongs all sovereignty and
praise and He is over all things, Omnipotent.*

*O Allah, no one prevent what You have willed to
bestow and no one can bestow what You have willed
to prevent and no wealth or majesty can benefit
anyone, as from You is all wealth and majesty.*[123]

5. To say:

«لَا إِلَهَ إِلَّا اللهُ وَحْدَهُ لَا شَرِيكَ لَهُ لَهُ الْمُلْكُ وَلَهُ الْحَمْدُ وَهُوَ
عَلَى كُلِّ شَيْءٍ قَدِيرٌ لَا حَوْلَ وَلَا قُوَّةَ إِلَّا بِاللهِ لَا إِلَهَ إِلَّا اللهُ
وَلَا نَعْبُدُ إِلَّا إِيَّاهُ لَهُ النِّعْمَةُ وَلَهُ الْفَضْلُ وَلَهُ الثَّنَاءُ الْحَسَنُ لَا إِلَهَ
إِلَّا اللهُ مُخْلِصِينَ لَهُ الدِّينَ وَلَوْ كَرِهَ الْكَافِرُونَ»

*There is no deity worthy of worship, except Allah alone,
having no partners. To Him belongs all sovereignty and
praise He is over all things, Omnipotent. There is no
might, or power, except with Allah. There is no deity
worthy of worship except Allah and We worship none,
except Him.*

*For Him is all favour, grace and glorious praise. There is
no deity worthy of worship, except Allah. We are sincere
in our faith to Him, even though the disbelievers dislike
it.*[134]

6. To say:

«اللَّهُمَّ أَعِنِّي عَلَى ذِكْرِكَ وَشُكْرِكَ وَحُسْنِ عِبَادَتِكَ»

*Allah, help me in Your remembrance and in gratitude to
You and in perfect worship of You.*[135]

7. To say:

«اللَّهُمَّ إِنِّي أَعُوذُ بِكَ مِنَ الْجُبْنِ وَأَعُوذُ بِكَ أَنْ أُرَدَّ إِلَى أَرْذَلِ
الْعُمُرِ وَأَعُوذُ بِكَ مِنْ فِتْنَةِ الدُّنْيَا وَأَعُوذُ بِكَ مِنْ عَذَابِ الْقَبْرِ»

O Allah, I seek refuge in Your from cowardice. And I seek refuge in You from returning to the worst part of my life. And I seek refuge in You from the trials of the Dunya. And I seek refuge in You from the punishment of the grave.[136]

8. To say:

«رَبِّ قِنِي عَذَابَكَ يَوْمَ تَبْعَثُ أَوْ تَجْمَعُ عِبَادَكَ»

'My Lord, save me from Your punishment of the Day when You resurrect or gather Your slaves'.

This is from the following *Hadeeth*, narrated by Al-Barraah (ﷺ) who said:

When we prayed behind the Messenger of Allah (ﷺ), we wished to be on his right so he would turn and face us after the prayer. And I heard him say,

«رَبِّ قِنِي عَذَابَكَ يَوْمَ تَبْعَثُ أَوْ تَجْمَعُ عِبَادَكَ»

'My Lord save me from Your punishment on the Day when You resurrect or gather together Your slaves'.[137]

9. To recite the last three *Suwar* of the Qur'aan:

﴿قُلْ هُوَ ٱللَّهُ أَحَدٌ﴾

"Say: 'He is Allah the One, the Unique...'"
(Al-Ikhlaas 112 :1 - 4)

﴿قُلْ أَعُوذُ بِرَبِّ ٱلْفَلَقِ﴾

"Say: 'I seek refuge with the Lord of the daybreak...'"
(Al-Falaq, 113 : 1 - 5)

﴿قُلْ أَعُوذُ بِرَبِّ ٱلنَّاسِ﴾

"Say: 'I seek refuge with the Lord of mankind...'"

(An-Naas, 114 : 1 - 6)

Repeat each *Soorah* three times, after the *Fajr* and *Maghrib* prayers. After all other obligatory prayers repeat them only once.[138]

10. To Recite *Aayah Al-Kursee* :

$$\langle\!\langle\ \dots\ \text{ٱللَّهُ لَآ إِلَٰهَ إِلَّا هُوَ ٱلْحَىُّ ٱلْقَيُّومُ}\ \rangle\!\rangle$$

"Allah, none has the right to be worshipped, but He, the Ever-Living..."

(Al-Baqarah, 2 :255)[139]

11. To say these supplications while in the place of prayer and not to change positions.[1] [140]

Benefits of these *Adhkaar* :

Some of the benefits of observing and preserving these *Sunan* after every obligatory prayer:

☐ If a Muslim preserves these supplications after every obligatory prayer then five hundred *Sadaqaat* are written for him, from the saying of the Prophet (ﷺ):

Every Tasbeeh is Sadaqah, every Takbeer is Sadaqah, every Tahmeed is Sadaqah and every Tahleel is Sadaqah.[141]

Imaam An-Nawawee said a person gains the reward as if he has paid this amount in charity.

☐ Five hundred trees will be planted for the Muslim

---

[1] The narrations that mention to supplicate in the place of prayer, refer to after *Salaah Al-Fajr* and *Al-Asr* only, and are therefore not applicable to other prayers. Readers should note that no narration was found to support this point.

who preserves these supplication after every prayer during the day and night:

The Messenger of Allah (ﷺ) passed by Aboo Hurayrah (ﷺ) while he was planting something and said:

'O Aboo Hurayrah, shall I not show you a planting better than this?'
He said:'Of course, O Messenger of Allah.'

He (ﷺ) said: 'say:...

«سُبْحَانَ اللهِ وَالْحَمْدُ للهِ وَلَا إِلَهَ إِلَّا اللهُ وَاللهُ أَكْبَرُ»

...subhaan allaah, al-hamdu lillaah, laa ilaaha illallaah, allaahu akbar...

...and a tree will be planted for you in Paradise for every one you say'.[142]

□ For the one who preserves the reading of *Aayah Al-Kursee* after every *Salaah*, there is nothing between him and entering Paradise, except death.[143]

□ Whoever preserves these praises will have his sins removed, even if they were as abundant as the foam on the sea.[144]

□ The one who preserves these praises after every prayer, will not be afflicted with failure or disgrace, in this world or the Hereafter:

The one who says the Mu'aqqibaat will not be afflicted with failure... and he mentioned these praises.[145]

□ It compensates for the lacking and deficiency in one's performance of the obligatory prayers.[146]

ADHKAAR OF THE MORNING AND EVENING

Some *Adhkaar* to be said in the morning and evening:

1. *Aayah Al-Kursee* :

﴿ٱللَّهُ لَآ إِلَٰهَ إِلَّا هُوَ ٱلْحَىُّ ٱلْقَيُّومُ . . . ﴾

"Allah, none has the right to be worshipped, but He, the Ever-Living..."

(Al-Baqarah, 2 :255)

From its benefits is:

Whoever says it in the morning will be protected from the jinn until evening, and whoever says it in the evening will be protected from them until the morning.[147]

2. *Al-Mu'awwidhaat* :

﴿قُلْ هُوَ ٱللَّهُ أَحَدٌ﴾

"Say:'He is Allah the One, the Unique...'"
(Al-Ikhlaas, 112 :1 - 4)

﴿قُلْ أَعُوذُ بِرَبِّ ٱلْفَلَقِ﴾

"Say:'I seek refuge with the Lord of daybreak...'"
(Al-Falaq, 113 :1 - 5)

﴿قُلْ أَعُوذُ بِرَبِّ ٱلنَّاسِ﴾

"Say: 'I seek refuge with the Lord of mankind...'"
(An-Naas, 114 :1 - 6)

From its benefits is that:

Whoever says them three times in the evening and morning, they will be sufficient for him in everything[1]

3. In <u>Saheeh</u> At-Targheeb Wa At-Tarheeb :

«يَا حَيُّ يَا قَيُّومُ بِرَحْمَتِكَ أَسْتَغِيثُ أَصْلِحْ لِي شَأْنِي كُلَّهُ وَلَا تَكِلْنِي إِلَى نَفْسِي طَرْفَةَ عَيْنٍ»

O Ever Living, O Self-Subsisting and Supporter of all, by Your mercy I seek assistance.

Rectify for me all of my affairs and do not leave me to myself, even for the blink of an eye.[149]

4. In <u>Saheeh</u> Muslim :

«أَمْسَيْنَا وَأَمْسَى الْمُلْكُ لِلَّهِ وَالْحَمْدُ لِلَّهِ، لَا إِلَهَ إِلَّا اللهُ وَحْدَهُ لَا شَرِيكَ لَهُ لَهُ الْمُلْكُ وَلَهُ الْحَمْدُ وَهُوَ عَلَى كُلِّ شَيْءٍ قَدِيرٌ، رَبِّ أَسْأَلُكَ خَيْرَ مَا فِي هَذِهِ اللَّيْلَةِ وَخَيْرَ مَا بَعْدَهَا وَأَعُوذُ بِكَ مِنْ شَرِّ مَا فِي هَذِهِ اللَّيْلَةِ وَشَرِّ مَا بَعْدَهَا رَبِّ أَعُوذُ بِكَ مِنَ الْكَسَلِ وَسُوءِ الْكِبَرِ رَبِّ أَعُوذُ بِكَ مِنْ عَذَابٍ فِي النَّارِ وَعَذَابٍ فِي الْقَبْرِ»

We have reached the evening (and at this very time) to Allah belongs all sovereignty, and all praise is for Allah.

None has the right to be worshipped, except Allah alone, having no partners.

---

[1] Sufficient for him in everthing means the person will be protected from all kinds of evil, as mentioned in *Tuhfat Al-Ahwadee* by Shaykh Mu<u>h</u>ammad Al-Mubaarakpuri.

To Him belongs all sovereignty and praise and He is over all things, Omnipotent.

My Lord, I ask You for the good of this night and the good of what follows it, and I seek refuge in You from the evil of this night and the evil of what follows it.

My Lord, I seek refuge in You from laziness and senility.

My Lord, I seek refuge in You from the torment of the Fire and the punishment of the grave.[150]

In the morning, replace

أَمْسَيْنَا وَأَمْسَى الْمُلْكُ لِلهِ

with الْيَوْمِ with اللَّيْلَةِ and replace أَصْبَحْنَا وَأَصْبَحَ الْمُلْكُ لِلهِ with

5. In *Sunan Aboo Daawood* and *At-Tirmidhee*:[151]

In the morning,

«اللَّهُمَّ بِكَ أَصْبَحْنَا، وَبِكَ أَمْسَيْنَا، وَبِكَ نَحْيَا، وَبِكَ نَمُوتُ
وَإِلَيْكَ الْمَصِيرُ».

O Allah, by Your leave we have reached the morning and by Your leave we have reached the evening and by Your leave we live and die and to You is our <u>destination</u>.

And in the evening,

«اللَّهُمَّ بِكَ أَمْسَيْنَا، وَبِكَ أَصْبَحْنَا، وَبِكَ نَحْيَا، وَبِكَ نَمُوتُ
وَإِلَيْكَ النُّشُورُ».

O Allah, by Your leave we have reached the evening and by Your leave we have reached the morning and by Your leave we live and die and to You is our <u>resurrection</u>.

6. In *Sunan ibn Maajah* :

«اللَّهُمَّ إِنِّي أَسْأَلُكَ عِلْمًا نَافِعًا، وَرِزْقًا طَيِّبًا، وَعَمَلًا مُتَقَبَّلًا» . (إذا أصبح)

O Allah, verily I ask You for knowledge that is beneficial, sustenance that is pure and actions that are acceptable. (To be said in the morning)[152]

7. In *Sunan At-Tirmidhee and others* :

«أَعُوذُ بِكَلِمَاتِ اللهِ التَّامَّاتِ مِنْ شَرِّ مَا خَلَقَ» .

I seek refuge in the perfect Words of Allah, from every evil created. (Three times in the evening)[153]

8. In *Sunan Aboo Daawood* :

«اللَّهُمَّ إِنِّي أَصْبَحْتُ أُشْهِدُكَ وَأُشْهِدُ حَمَلَةَ عَرْشِكَ، وَمَلَائِكَتَكَ وَجَمِيعَ خَلْقِكَ، أَنَّكَ أَنْتَ اللهُ لَا إِلَهَ إِلَّا أَنْتَ وَحْدَكَ لَا شَرِيكَ لَكَ، وَأَنَّ مُحَمَّدًا عَبْدُكَ وَرَسُولُكَ» . (أربع مرات)

O Allah, verily, I have reached the morning and I call on You, the bearers of Your throne, Your angels and all of Your creation witness that You are Allah.

None has the right to be worshipped, except You, alone, having no partner and that Muhammad (ﷺ) is Your servant and Messenger. (Four times)[154]

From its benefits, is that whoever says it in the morning or evening four times, Allah will free him from the Fire.

In the evening, say:

اللَّهُمَّ إِنِّي أَمْسَيْتُ

in the place of

اللَّهُمَّ إِنِّي أَصْبَحْتُ

9. In *Sunan Aboo Daawood and Musnad Imaam Ahmad :*

«اللَّهُمَّ عَافِنِي فِي بَدَنِي، اللَّهُمَّ عَافِنِي فِي سَمْعِي، اللَّهُمَّ عَافِنِي فِي بَصَرِي، لَا إِلَهَ إِلَّا أَنْتَ» . (ثلاثَ مراتٍ)

O Allah, grant my body health.

O Allah, grant my hearing health.

O Allah, grant my sight health.
No one has the right to be worshipped, except You.
(Three times). [155]

10. From the same *Hadeeth :* [156]

«اللَّهُمَّ إِنِّي أَعُوذُ بِكَ مِنَ الْكُفْرِ وَالْفَقَرِ اللَّهُمَّ إِنِّي أَعُوذُ بِكَ مِنْ عَذَابِ الْقَبْرِ، لَا إِلَهَ إِلَّا أَنْتَ» . (ثلاثَ مرات)

O Allah, I seek refuge in You from disbelief and poverty.

O Allah, I seek refuge in You from the punishment of the grave.

No one has the right to be worshipped, except You.
(Three times)

Both of the above supplication come in the same narration. They have been separated because in the Hadeeth they did not come as one single supplication. They are to be read three times each in the morning and evening.

11. In <u>Saheeh</u> Al-Bukhaaree:

«اللَّهُمَّ أَنْتَ رَبِّي لَا إِلَهَ إِلَّا أَنْتَ، خَلَقْتَنِي وَأَنَا عَبْدُكَ، وَأَنَا
عَلَى عَهْدِكَ وَوَعْدِكَ مَا اسْتَطَعْتُ، أَعُوذُ بِكَ مِنْ شَرِّ مَا
صَنَعْتُ، أَبُوءُ لَكَ بِنِعْمَتِكَ عَلَيَّ، وَأَبُوءُ بِذَنْبِي فَاغْفِرْ لِي فَإِنَّهُ لَا
يَغْفِرُ الذُّنُوبَ إِلَّا أَنْتَ».

*O Allah, You are my Lord; none has the right to be
worshipped, except You. You created me and I am
Your servant and I abide by Your covenant and
promise as best as I can.*

*I seek refuge in You from the evil of what I have
committed. I acknowledge Your favour on me and I
acknowledge my sin, so forgive me, for verily no one
can forgive sins, except You.[157]*

From its benefits is that whoever says it, having full
conviction in it, and dies during the night will enter
Paradise; likewise, if he says it and dies during the
day he will enter Paradise, as narrated in the same
<u>Hadeeth</u>.

12. Narrated by Imaam A<u>h</u>mad in his *Musnad*:

«أَصْبَحْنَا عَلَى فِطْرَةِ الْإِسْلَام وَعَلَى كَلِمَةِ الْإِخْلَاصِ، وَعَلَى
دِينِ نَبِيِّنَا مُحَمَّدٍ (ﷺ)، وَعَلَى مِلَّةِ أَبِينَا إِبْرَاهِيمَ، حَنِيفًا مُسْلِمًا
وَمَا كَانَ مِنَ الْمُشْرِكِينَ».

*We rise (awake) on the Fitrah of Islam and the word of
pure faith and on the religion of our Prophet Mu<u>h</u>ammad
(ﷺ) and the religion of our forefather, Ibraaheem, who*

was a Muslim and of true faith, and was not of those who associated others with Allah.[158]

13. From *Amal Al-Yawm Wa Al-Laylah* of *An-Nasaaee'*:

«اللَّهُمَّ مَا أَصْبَحَ بِي مِنْ نِعْمَةٍ أَوْ بِأَحَدٍ مِنْ خَلْقِكَ فَمِنْكَ وَحْدَكَ لَا شَرِيكَ لَكَ، فَلَكَ الْحَمْدُ وَلَكَ الشُّكْرُ».

O Allah, whatever blessing I, or any of Your creation has awoken on, is from You alone, having no partners, so for You alone is all praise and to You alone is all thanks.[159]

From its benefits is that whoever said this in the morning has fulfilled his gratitude to Allah for the day, and whoever says it in the evening has fulfilled his gratitude to Allah for the night, as narrated in the same *Hadeeth*.

14. In *Sunan Aboo Daawood*:

﴿حَسْبِيَ ٱللَّهُ لَآ إِلَٰهَ إِلَّا هُوَ عَلَيْهِ تَوَكَّلْتُ وَهُوَ رَبُّ ٱلْعَرْشِ ٱلْعَظِيمِ﴾

Allah is sufficient for me. No one has the right to be worshipped, except Him. On Him I place my trust and He is the Lord of the great throne. (Seven times)[160]

From its benefits is that whoever says it seven times in the morning and the evening, Allah will suffice for him all of his important affairs related to his worldly matters and to his religious matters (i.e. the Hereafter).

15. In *Sunan Aboo Daawood* and other collections:

«بِسْمِ اللهِ الَّذِي لَا يَضُرُّ مَعَ اسْمِهِ شَيْءٌ فِي الْأَرْضِ وَلَا فِي السَّمَاءِ وَهُوَ السَّمِيعُ الْعَلِيمُ».

In the Name of Allah, with whose Name nothing is harmed on the earth or in the heavens and He is the All-Seeing, the All-Knowing. (Three times)[161]

From its benefits is that whoever says it three times in the morning and three times in the evening nothing will harm him.

16. In *Sunan Aboo Daawood*, *Musnad Imaam Ahmad* and in other collections:

«رَضِيتُ بِاللهِ رَبًّا، وَبِالْإِسْلَامِ دِينًا، وَبِمُحَمَّدٍ نَبِيًّا». (ثلاث مرات)

I am pleased with Allah as a Lord, and Islaam as a religion and Muhammad (ﷺ) as a Prophet. (Three times)[162]

From its benefits is that whoever reads this supplication three times in the morning and in the evening, has the right that Allah suffices him on Day of Standing (i.e. the Day of Resurrection), as mentioned in the same *Hadeeth*.

17. In *Saheeh* Muslim :

«أَسْتَغْفِرُ اللهَ وَأَتُوبُ إِلَيْهِ». (مائة مرة)

I ask Allah for forgivness and to Him I repent. (One hundred times in the day)[163]

18. Also, in *Saheeh* Muslim :

«سُبْحَانَ اللهِ وَبِحَمْدِهِ: عَدَدَ خَلْقِهِ، وَرِضَا نَفْسِهِ، وَزِنَةَ عَرْشِهِ
وَمِدَادَ كَلِمَاتِهِ». (ثلاث مرات)

*Far removed is Allah from any imperfections and I
praise Him by the number of His creation and His
pleasure and by the weight of His throne and the ink of
His Words. (Three times)*[164]

19. Also, in <u>S</u>aheeh Muslim :

«سُبْحَانَ اللهِ وَبِحَمْدِهِ» (مائة مرة)

*Far removed is Allah from any imperfections and I
praise Him. (One hundred times)*[165]

From its benefits is that whoever says it one
hundred times, in the morning and in the evening,
no one will come on the Day of Resurrection with
greater than what he has, except the person who has
said the same as what he has, or more than him.[1]

Another benefit is that it removes sins, even if they
are as much as the foam on the sea.[166]

20. In <u>S</u>aheeh Al- Bukhaaree and *Muslim*:

«لَا إِلٰهَ إِلَّا اللهُ وَحْدَهُ لَا شَرِيكَ لَهُ، لَهُ الْمُلْكُ وَلَهُ الْحَمْدُ وَهُوَ
عَلَى كُلِّ شَيْءٍ قَدِيرٌ» (مائة مرة)

There is no deity worthy of worship, except Allah

---

[1] This is applicable to the one who says these praises:
(a) at the right time, i.e. before sunrise and sunset,
(b) with sincerity, conscious of what is being said and
reflecting on the meaning and
(c) with consistency.

alone, having no partners. To Him belongs all sovereignty and praise, and He is over all things Omnipotent. (One hundred times)[167]

Whoever says this one hundred times in the day will have the reward of:

- Freeing ten slaves,
- On hundred good deeds being written for him,
- One hundred sins being removed and
- Being protected during that day, until the evening, from the *Shaytaan*.

21. In *Saheeh Al-Kalimaat At-Tayyib*:

«اللَّهُمَّ عَالِمَ الْغَيْبِ وَالشَّهَادَةِ فَاطِرَ السَّمْوَاتِ وَالْأَرْضِ، رَبَّ كُلِّ شَيْءٍ وَمَلِيكَهُ، أَشْهَدُ أَنْ لَا إِلَهَ إِلَّا أَنْتَ، أَعُوذُ بِكَ مِنْ شَرِّ نَفْسِي، وَمِنْ شَرِّ الشَّيْطَانِ وَشِرْكِهِ، وَأَنْ أَقْتَرِفَ عَلَى نَفْسِي سُوءًا، أَوْ أَجُرَّهُ إِلَى مُسْلِمٍ».

O Allah, Knower of the unseen and the seen, Creator of the Heavens and the Earth, Lord and Sovereign of all things. I bear witness there is no deity worthy of worship, except You.

I seek refuge in You from the evil of my soul and from the evil and Shirki[1] *of Shaytaan, and from*

---

[1] There are two opinions on how this should be pronounced:
(a) The first opinion is that the word should be pronounced as *Shiraki*, which means plots and plans. So, this part of the supplication would read,
I seek refuge in Your from the evil of my soul and from the evil and plans of Shytaan.

*committing wrong against my soul, or the like of that,
to another Muslim.*[1] 168

Points to note:

☐ Whenever one of these supplications is mentioned,
one of the *Sunan* is implemented. It is necessary for a
Muslim to take care of reading these supplications in
the morning and evening so that one implements as
much as possible of these *Sunan*.

☐ It is also necessary that you repeat these
supplications with sincerity, truthfulness and
having certainty in them. Try to be conscious of
their meanings so that they affect you in your life,
morals and conduct.

(b) The second opinion, which seems to be the strongest, is
that it should be pronounced as *Shirki*; this refers to whatever
the *Shaytaan* is calling you towards, in terms of acts of
worship, which result in associating partners with Allah. It
does not meant that *Shirk* is being committed by *Shaytaan*
himself. On the contrary it is the person who commits the
Shirk in obedience to *Shaytaan*.

For a more detailed explanation, refer to *Tuhfat Al-Ahwadee*,
Volume 9, *Hadeeth* 3452, by Shaykh Muhammad Al-
Mubaarakpuri.

[1] Shaykh Al-Albaanee mentioned that the last part,
...is from another narration is *Sunan At-Tirmidhee*, narrated by
'Abdullah bin 'Ammaar, and is not mentioned as part of this
supplication, which is also from *Sunan At-Tirmidhee*, but
narrated by Aboo Hurayrah.

MEETING PEOPLE

From the *Sunan* of meeting a Muslim, are the following:

1. Give *Tasleem* :

The Messenger of Allah (ﷺ) was asked:

'Which Islam is good (in terms of actions)?' He said: 'To feed the people and to say Salaam to those you know and those you do not know.'[169]

2. Lengthen the greeting:

A man entered upon the Messenger of Allah (ﷺ) and said:

«السَّلَامُ عَلَيْكُمْ»

'As-salaamu alaykum.'

The Messenger (ﷺ) replied to the Salaam. Then the man sat down and the Messenger (ﷺ) said: 'Ten'. Then another man came and said:

«السَّلَامُ عَلَيْكُمْ وَرَحْمَةُ اللهِ »

'As-salaamu alaykum wa rahmatullah.'

The Messenger (ﷺ) replied. Then the man sat down and the Messenger (ﷺ) said: 'Twenty'. The another man came and said:

«السَّلَامُ عَلَيْكُمْ وَرَحْمَةُ اللهِ وَبَرَكَاتُهُ»

'As-salaamu alaykum wa rahumatullaahi wa

barakaatuh.'

The Messenger (ﷺ) replied. Then the man sat down and the Messsenger (ﷺ) said: 'Thirty'.[170]

Look at how much loss of reward a person inflicts on himself by sufficing himself with saying only a part of the salutation. The person should say the entire *Salaam* so that he attains thirty good deeds. The least reward for a good deed is ten times its like; therefore, by saying the full greeting, one can earn three hundred good deeds or more.

Accustom yourself to completing the *Salaam* up to *Barakaatuh* (بركاته) to obtain this great reward.

The Muslim says the *Salaam* many times during the day. He says it when entering the *Masjid* to the people sitting and when leaving them,[1] entering and leaving his house etc.

Do not forget that it is also from the *Sunnah* that whoever decides to leave a person that he should say the complete *Salaam:*

When one of you comes to a gathering, then say: 'Salaam,' and if someone decides to leave, then say:'Salaam,' and the first does not have more right than the last.[2] [171]

---

[1] No evidence for saying the *Salaam* when entering or leaving the *Masjid* was found. However, what is confirmed in the *Sunnah* is to pray two *Rak'ah* of *Tahiyaat Al-Masjid* on entering.

[2] i.e. it is as important to give the *Salaam* when leaving a gathering, as it is when entering it. So, one does not have more right than the other.

3. Smile, as the Prophet (ﷺ) said:

> Do not consider any of the good things as insignificant – even if it is that you meet your brother with a cheerful face.[172]

4. Shake hands, as the Prophet (ﷺ) said:

> There are not two Muslims who meet each other and shake hands, except that they are forgiven before they depart (from each other).[173]

Imaam An-Nawawee said:

> Know that this shaking of hands is preferred with every meeting.[1]

Notice that if you shake hands with whomever you meet, greet them with *Salaam* and smile at them you would have fulfilled three *Sunan* at once.

5. Say a *Kalimah Tayyibah*:

$$﴿وَقُل لِّعِبَادِى يَقُولُوا۟ ٱلَّتِى هِىَ أَحْسَنُ إِنَّ ٱلشَّيْطَٰنَ يَنزَغُ بَيْنَهُمْ إِنَّ ٱلشَّيْطَٰنَ كَانَ لِلْإِنسَٰنِ عَدُوًّا مُّبِينًا﴾$$

> "Say to my Slaves to say that which is better. Verily, Shaytaan incites to evil between them. Verily, Shaytaan is for mankind a clear enemy."
>
> (Al-Israa', 17: 53)

The Prophet (ﷺ) said:

> A Kalimah Tayyibah is charity.[174]

Kalimah Tayyibah includes the remembrance of Allah, supplication, *Salaam*, praising someone for their good

---

[1] It is not permissible to shake hands with a non-*Mahram*.

traits, noble character, good manners and actions.

A *Kalimah* *Tayyibah* has a powerful affect on a person –
it brings peace and tranquillity to a person's soul and
puts serenity into his heart. It is evidence of what is in
the heart of the believer of light, guidance and proof of
being of the right path.

Have you thought, my dear brother, to fill your life–
from the morning to the evening – with kind words, to
your spouse, children, neighbours, friends, co-workers
and whomever else you deal with, who maybe in need
of such words?

EATING

Observe the following *Sunan* for eating:

1. Pronounce the *Tasmiyah* :

«بِسْمِ اللهِ»

In the Name of Allah.

2. Eat with the right hand.

3. Eat from what is in front of you.

These three *Sunan* are recorded in one *Hadeeth*:

O young man, mention the Name of Allah, eat with your right and eat from what is in front of you.[1] 175

4. If some food drops, clean it and then eat it:

*If one of you dropped a morsel of food, then remove from it whatever there is of dirt and then eat it...*176

5. Eat with three fingers.

The Prophet (ﷺ) used to eat with three fingers. This was his (ﷺ) way of eating and is better, unless a need requires otherwise.177

6. The etiquette of sitting when eating:

- • Kneel on one's shins and front of the feet, or

- • Keep the right leg upright and sit on the left.

This is what is preferred, as was mentioned by Al-Haafidh Ibn Hajar in *Fath Al-Baaree*.

---

[1] i.e. near to you.

Observe the following *Sunan* after eating:

1. Lick the bowl and the fingers:
   The Prophet (ﷺ) ordered the licking of the fingers and bowl, and he said:

   Verily, You do not know in which of it (i.e. which morsel of food) is the blessing.[178]

2. Praise Allah:

   Verily, Allah is pleased with the slave who eats his food and praises Allah for it...[179]

And the supplication of the Prophet ﷺ is:

«الْحَمْدُ لله الَّذِي أَطْعَمَنِي هَذَا، وَرَزَقَنِيهِ، مِنْ غَيْرِ حَوْلٍ مِنِّي وَلَا قُوَّةٍ».

All praise is for Allaah, who fed me this and provided it for me without any might or power from myself.

From the benefits of this *Du'aa*, is that:

The person's past sins will be forgiven.[180]

DRINKING

From the *Sunan* of drinking is:

1. Pronounce the *Tasmiyah* :

«بِسْمِ اللهِ»

In the Name of Allah.

2. Drink with the right hand:

O young man, mention the Name of Allah, eat with your right..[1] 181

3. When drinking, breathe outside of the vessel. And do not drink all at once, but rather, take three breaths.182

4. Sit while drinking:

*Let not one of you drink standing...*183

5. Say *Tahmeed* after drinking:

*Verily, Allah is pleased with the slave who eats his food and praises Him for it... and he who drinks and praises Him for it.*184

---

[1] This *Hadeeth* does not explicitly mention drinking with the right hand. However, there is a narration of Muslim, on the authority of Ibn 'Umar ( ):

When one of you eats, let him eat with his right hand ; and when he drinks, let him drink with his right hand – because the Shaytaan eats and drinks with his left hand.

Saheeh Muslim, The Book Of Drinks, *Hadeeth* 2020.

PERFORMING VOLUNTARY PRAYERS AT HOME

Regarding the excellence of praying at home, the Prophet (ﷺ) said:

> *Verily, the best prayer of a person is in his house, except for the obligatory prayer.* [185]

Also, from the *Hadeeth* where the Prophet (ﷺ) said:

> *The voluntary prayer of a man (in a place) where no person can see him is equal to twenty-five times his prayer where people can see him.* [186]

In another *Hadeeth*, the Prophet (ﷺ) said:

> *The superiority of the prayer of a man in his house over his prayer (in a place) so that the people can see him, is like the superiority of the obligatory over the voluntary.* [187]

This *Sunnah* is repeated many times during the day and night. It includes prayers like *Sunnah Ar-Rawaatib*, *Salaah Ad-Duhaa* and *Al-Witr*.

For every one of these, the person should observe the prayers in his house in order to increase his reward and fulfil the *Sunnah*.

Implementing these voluntary prayers in the house is a means to:

☐ Perfecting tranquillity and sincerity.

☐ Distance oneself from showing off.

☐ Have mercy descend on the house.

☐ Cause the *Shaytaan* to leave.

☐ Multiply the reward of the voluntary prayer, just as the reward of the obligatory prayer is multiplied by performing it in the *Masjid*.

LEAVING A GATHERING

Say the *Du'aa* for atonement of the gathering:

«سُبْحَانَكَ اللَّهُمَّ وَبِحَمْدِكَ، أَشْهَدُ أَنْ لَا إِلَهَ إِلَّا أَنْتَ،
أَسْتَغْفِرُكَ وَأَتُوبُ إِلَيْكَ» .

Far removed are You from any imperfections, O Allah and I praise You.

I bear witness that there is no deity worthy of worship except You.

I seek Your forgiveness and to You I repent.[188]

A Muslim attends many gathering during the course of the day and night. Here are a few examples:

- ☐ When you eat, no doubt you will speak with whoever is sitting with you.

- ☐ When you see a person who is your friend or neighbour, you would speak to them, even if you were standing.

- ☐ When sitting, for example at work, school or place of study, and some of your friends or colleagues are with you.

- ☐ When sitting with your wife and children and you are conversing with them and they with you.

- ☐ When you are on a journey or on the way to a place in the car and you are talking with whoever is with you, whether your wife or children.

- ☐ In a public lecture or private lesson.

Notice how many times you mention this *Du'aa* during the day and night. In this way, you continually maintain a connection with Allah.

How many times do you praise your Lord, declare Him free of anything not befitting Him and glorify Him, when you say:

Far removed are You from any imperfections, O Allah and I praise You.

How many times have you acknowledged the Oneness[1] of Allah the Most High, in His Lordship, Worship and Names and Attributes, when you say:

I bear witness that there is no deity worthy of worship except You.

How many times have you renewed your repentance and forgiveness with Your Lord in the day and night, from that which you have done or earned in that gathering, when you say:

I Seek Your forgiveness and to You I repent.

So, during the day and night, you are between confirming the Oneness of Allah while negating what does not belong to Him, and seeking His forgiveness and repentance for that which you have earned of wrong-doings.

From the benefits of implementing this *Sunnah*:

□ It is redemption for sins and mistakes you may have

---

[1] Oneness means to believe that Allah (ﷻ) is alone, unique and no-one shares with Him in the three issues mentioned (i.e. His Lordship, Worship or Names and Attributes).

spoken in that gathering.

Ibn Al-Qayyim said the gathering of Muslims is of two types:

☐ A social gathering to occupy time. This is more detrimental than beneficial and to a lesser extent it corrupts the heart and wastes time.

☐ A gathering on cooperating on means of success and advising to truth. This is of the greatest treasures and most beneficial.

MAKING THE CORRECT INTENTION

Have the correct intention:

Verily, actions are judged by intentions and every person gets the reward of what he intended...[189]

Important point:

Know, that all permissible action, like sleeping, eating, working and other than these, can be changed into acts of obedience and a means of nearness to Allah. One can obtain many good deeds due to these actions, <u>if they have the intention of drawing close to Allah when doing them</u>. For example, if you go to sleep early, so you can wake up for *Qiyaam Al-Layl* or *Salaah Al-Fajr*, then this sleeping becomes an act of worship. This is true for all other permissible actions.

COMBINING MULTIPLE
ACTS OF WORSHIP

The way to utilize a single opportunity to perform multiple acts of worship is only known to those who know how to manage their time.

Here are some examples:

☐ When you go to the *Masjid*, either walking or by car, this act of going is worship, in and of itself and you will be rewarded for this. But, it is also possible to utilize the same time in remembrance of Allah *(Dhikr)* or recitation of the Qur'an. Hence, a single opportunity has been utilized to perform multiple acts of worship.

☐ When going to a *Waleemah* that is free from evil acts, this attendance is an act of worship itself. But, it is possible to also utilize the time to call people to Allah or to engage in the remembrance of Allah *(Dhikr)*,

☐ For a lady to remain at home and perform household chores is itself an act of worship, if she intends to get close to Allah by this. It is also possible for her to utilize this time with other acts of worship, like *Dhikr* or listening to an Islamic tape.

On the authority of Ibn 'Umar (ﷺ) who said:

While in a sitting with the Messenger of Allah ﷺ, we counted that he said,

«رَبِّ اغْفِرْ لِي وَتُبْ عَلَيَّ إِنَّكَ أَنْتَ التَّوَّابُ الرَّحِيمُ» .

O Allah, forgive me and I repent to You.

Verily, You are the most forgiving, the most Mercifyl.[190]

... one hundred times.

Ponder on how the Prophet (ﷺ) took a single opportunity to perform two acts of worship:

○ The remembrance of Allah and seeking of His forgiveness and

○ Sitting with the companions and teaching them the dictates of their religion.

REMEMBERING ALLAH
AT ALL TIMES

Points to note regarding *Dhikr* of Allah:

1. *Dhikr* is the foundation of the worship of Allah. It is the link of the worshipper with his Creator, in all times and conditions. On the authority of 'Aishah (🏵) who said:

The Messenger (ﷺ) remembered Allah at all times.[191]

This connection with Allah is life, resorting to Him is salvation, nearness to Him is success and pleasure and being far from Him is misguidance and loss.

2. *Dhikr* distinguishes a believer from a hypocrite, as one of the characteristics of the hypocrites is that they do not remember Allah, except a little:

﴿ . . . وَلَا يَذْكُرُونَ ٱللَّهَ إِلَّا قَلِيلًا ﴾

"*... and they do not remember Allah except a little.*"

(An-Nisaa', 3 :142)

3. *Shaytaan* does not triumph over the people unless they are heedless of the *Dhikr* of Allah. The *Dhikr* of Allah is an impregnable shield. A person can take sanctuary in it from the plots of *Shaytaan*. *Shaytaan* loves for a person to forget the *Dhikr* of Allah.

4. *Dhikr* is a means to happiness:

﴿ ٱلَّذِينَ ءَامَنُوا۟ وَتَطْمَئِنُّ قُلُوبُهُم بِذِكْرِ ٱللَّهِ أَلَا بِذِكْرِ ٱللَّهِ تَطْمَئِنُّ ٱلْقُلُوبُ ﴾

"*Those who believe and whose hearts find rest in the*

remembrance of Allah, verily, in the remembrance of Allah do hearts find rest."

(Ar-Ra'd, 13:28)

5. Remember Allah continuously.

The people of Paradise will not regret anything except an hour that passed them in the world in which they did not remember Allah, the Great and the Almighty. Remembering Allah continuously, results in a continuous connection with Him.

In this regard, Imaam An-Nawawee said:

The scholars are unanimous on the permissibility of Dhikr with the heart and on the tongue for the ritually impure, menstruating women and during postnatal bleeding, by saying Tasbeeh Tahmeed, Takbeer, Tahleel, as well as Salaah on the Messenger of Allah (ﷺ) and other supplications. There is a difference of opinion about reciting the Qur'an.

6. Allah remembers the one who remembers Him. Whoever remembers his Lord, the Great and Almighty, He will remember him:

﴿فَٱذۡكُرُونِیۤ أَذۡكُرۡكُمۡ وَٱشۡكُرُواْ لِی وَلَا تَكۡفُرُونِ﴾

"Remember me and I will remember you and be grateful to Me and never be ungrateful to Me."

(Al-Baqarah, 2:152)

A person would be extremely happy if it was conveyed to him that the ruler of land mentioned him his gathering and praised him. So, how would he feel if Allah, the Most High, Lord of the Worlds, mentioned him in a gathering, better than this?

7. What is not meant by the remembrance of Allah is muttering a word or words, while the heart is neglectful of what is being said and unmindful of Allah's exaltation and His obedience.

So, remembrance with the tongue is undoubtedly associated with reflection and influence from the meanings of words.

﴿وَٱذۡكُر رَّبَّكَ فِي نَفۡسِكَ تَضَرُّعٗا وَخِيفَةٗ وَدُونَ ٱلۡجَهۡرِ مِنَ ٱلۡقَوۡلِ بِٱلۡغُدُوِّ وَٱلۡأٓصَالِ وَلَا تَكُن مِّنَ ٱلۡغَٰفِلِينَ﴾

"And remember your Lord within yourself, humbly and with fear and without loudness in words, in the mornings and the afternoons, and be not of those who are neglectful."

(Al-A'raaf, 7:205)

It is necessary that the person who is remembering Allah should understand what he is saying – he should combine the remembrance of the heart with that of the tongue so that he is attached to his Lord both outwardly and inwardly.

REFLECTING ON THE BLESSINGS OF ALLAH

Constantly remember the blessings of Allah, as the Prophet (ﷺ) said:

Reflect on the blessings of Allah and do not reflect about Allah.[1] 192

From the things that are repeated by a Muslim during the day and night, is the recognition of the favours of Allah on him — how many situations are there?

How many events are there that a person sees and hears during the day and night that require him to reflect and ponder on the favours of Allah and require him to praise Him as a result?

Have you not realised the favours of Allah on you, when you are going to the *Masjid* and you see how the people around you have been deprived of this favour? This is especially true at the time of *Salaah Al-Fajr* and the Muslims are in their houses in a deep sleep, as if they were dead.

Have you not realised the favours of Allah on you when you walk along the road and witness different sights – this one has had car accident, that one has raised the sound of *Shaytaan* (i.e. music and songs) in his car and son on?

Have you not realised the favours of Allah on you, when you listen to or read the news about events

---

[1] i.e. do not reflect on those things that humans cannot understand, like the reality of Allah's Attributes etc.

occurring in the world, like famines, floods, the spreading of diseases, disasters, earthquakes, wars, homelessness and the like?

Indeed, the worshipper of Allah is fortunate – he is the one whose heart, feelings and perceptions are aware of the favours of Allah on him in all situations and circumstances.

He continues to praise, thank and glorify Him due to what he is enjoying from His bounties, like the blessings of the religion, health, prosperity or being away from evil.

In a narration, Prophet (ﷺ) said:

Whoever sees someone in affliction and says:

«الْحَمْدُ لِلّهِ الَّذِي عَافَانِي مِمَّا ابْتَلَاكَ بِهِ وَفَضَّلَنِي عَلَى كَثِيرٍ مِمَّنْ خَلَقَ تَفْضِيلًا».

'All praise is for Allah, the One who saved me from that which He has tested you with and Who has favoured me over much of His creation,' would not be afflicted with that trial[1] 193

Allah (ﷻ) says:

﴿. . . فَٱذْكُرُوٓاْ ءَالَآءَ ٱللَّهِ لَعَلَّكُمْ تُفْلِحُونَ﴾

"... so, remember the graces (bestowed on you) from Allah, so that you may be grateful."

(Al-A'raaf, 7:69)

---

[1] It should be said quietly so that the person afflicted cannot hear.

COMPLETING THE QUR'AN
EVERY MONTH

Complete the reading of the Qur'an every month, for the Prophet (ﷺ) said:

Complete the reading of the Qur'an every month.[194]

The method of completing the reading of the Qur'an every month is to go approximately ten minutes early to the *Masjid* for the obligatory prayer. It is possible to read two pages, or four sides, in this time before the prayer. So, during the day, it would amount to ten pages, or twenty sides, and this is a complete *Juz'*. In this way, you can complete the Qur'an every month with ease.

BEFORE GOING TO SLEEP

From the *Sunan* of going to sleep, is:

1. Say the supplication for going to sleep:

«بِاسْمِكِ اللَّهُمَّ أَمُوتُ وَأَحْيَا».

In your Name, O Allah, I die and live.[195]

2. Recite the *Mu'awwidhaat* and wipe the body:

The Prophet (ﷺ) cupped his hands together and Yanfuth[1] in them and then read:

﴿قُلْ هُوَ ٱللَّهُ أَحَدٌ﴾

"Say:'He is Allah the One, the Unique...'"
(Al-Ikhlaas, 112 : 1 - 4)

﴿قُلْ أَعُوذُ بِرَبِّ ٱلْفَلَقِ﴾

"Say: 'I seek refuge with the Lord of the daybreak...'"
(Al-Falaq, 113 : 1 - 5)

﴿قُلْ أَعُوذُ بِرَبِّ ٱلنَّاسِ﴾

"Say : 'I seek refuge with the Lord of mankind...'"
(An-Naas, 114 : 1 - 6)

... and then he would wipe whatever he was able to of his body with his hands, beginning with the head and face and then the remaining parts of the body.

He would do this three times.[196]

------

[1] See: Glossary of Terms, for an explanation of this word.

3. The last two *Ayaat* of *Soorah Al-Baqarah* :

$$\text{﴾} \ldots \text{إِلَيْهِ أُنزِلَ بِمَآ ٱلرَّسُولُ ءَامَنَ﴿}$$

"The Messenger believes in what has been sent down to him..."

(Al-Baqarah, 2 : 285 - 6)

This is taken from the <u>H</u>adeeth :

Whoever reads them (i.e. the last two Verses) at night they will be <u>Kafataa</u> for him.[197]

Imaam An-Nawawee said:

The scholars have differed as to the meaning of <u>Kafataa</u>. It is said that it means they are sufficient for him regarding the Night Prayer and it was also said it means they are sufficient in protection from every evil, misfortune and harm. I say that both of these meanings are acceptable...

4. Recite *Aayah Al-Kursee* :

$$\text{﴾} \ldots \text{ٱلْقَيُّومُ ٱلْحَىُّ هُوَ إِلَّا إِلَهَ لَا ٱللَّهُ﴿}$$

"Allah, none has the right to be worshipped, but He, the Ever-Living..."

(Al-Baqarah, 2 : 225)

From the benefits of reciting this, is that:

For whoever reads it, there would remain a protection over him from Allah and Shay<u>t</u>aan would not come close to him.[198]

There are many supplications and *Adhkaar* that can be said at the time of going to sleep, like:

1. In <u>S</u>a<u>h</u>ee<u>h</u> Al-Bukhaaree and *Muslim* :

«بِاسْمِكَ رَبِّي وَضَعْتُ جَنْبِي، وَبِكَ أَرْفَعُهُ، فَإِنْ أَمْسَكْتَ نَفْسِي
فَارْحَمْهَا، وَإِنْ أَرْسَلْتَهَا فَاحْفَظْهَا، بِمَا تَحْفَظُ بِهِ عِبَادَكَ
الصَّالِحِينَ».

*In Your Name, my Lord, I lie down, and in Your
Name, I rise.
So, if You take my soul then have mercy on it.*

*And if You return it, then protect it in the manner
you have protected (the souls of) Your righteous
servants.*[199]

2. In <u>S</u>a<u>h</u>ee<u>h</u> Al-Kalimaat At-<u>T</u>ayyib :

«اللَّهُمَّ عَالِمَ الْغَيْبِ وَالشَّهَادَةِ فَاطِرَ السَّمٰوَاتِ وَالْأَرْضِ، رَبَّ
كُلِّ شَيْءٍ وَمَلِيكَهُ، أَشْهَدُ أَنْ لَا إِلَهَ إِلَّا أَنْتَ، أَعُوذُ بِكَ مِنْ شَرِّ
نَفْسِي، وَمِنْ شَرِّ الشَّيْطَانِ وَشِرْكِهِ، وَأَنْ أَقْتَرِفَ عَلَى نَفْسِي
سُوءًا، أَوْ أَجُرَّهُ إِلَى مُسْلِمٍ».

*O Allah, Knower of the unseen and the seen, Creator
of the Heavens and the Earth, Lord and Sovereign of
all things. I bear witness that there is no deity worthy
of worship, except You.
I seek refuge in You from the evil of my soul and from
the evil and*[1] *of Shay<u>t</u>aan. And from committing
wrong against my soul, or the like of that, to another
Mulim.*[200]

3. In <u>S</u>a<u>h</u>ee<u>h</u> Al-Bukhaaree and *Muslim* :

---

[1] See: *Adhkaar* Of The Morning And Evening, footnote 1.

«اللَّهُمَّ أَسْلَمْتُ نَفْسِي إِلَيْكَ، وَفَوَّضْتُ أَمْرِي إِلَيْكَ، وَوَجَّهْتُ وَجْهِي إِلَيْكَ، وَأَلْجَأْتُ ظَهْرِي إِلَيْكَ، رَغْبَةً وَرَهْبَةً إِلَيْكَ، لَا مَلْجَأَ وَلَا مَنْجَا مِنْكَ إِلَّا إِلَيْكَ، آمَنْتُ بِكِتَابِكَ الَّذِي أَنْزَلْتَ وَبِنَبِيِّكَ الَّذِي أَرْسَلْتَ».

O Allah, I submit my soul to You, and I entrust my affair to You, and I turn my face to You, and I totally rely on You, in hope and fear.
There is neither refuge nor safe heaven from You, except with You. I believe in Your Book that You revealed and in the Prophet You sent.[201]

4. In *Saheeh* Muslim :

«اللَّهُمَّ إِنَّكَ خَلَقْتَ نَفْسِي وَأَنْتَ تَوَفَّاهَا، لَكَ مَمَاتُهَا وَمَحْيَاهَا، إِنْ أَحْيَيْتَهَا فَاحْفَظْهَا، وَإِنْ أَمَتَّهَا فَاغْفِرْ لَهَا. اللَّهُمَّ إِنِّي أَسْأَلُكَ الْعَافِيَةَ».

O Allah, You have created my soul and You shall take its life. To You belongs its life and death. If You should keep my soul alive, then protect it. And if You should take it, then forgive it. O Allah, I ask You to grant me good health.[202]

5. In *Sunan Aboo Daawood* and *At-Tirmidhee* :

«اللَّهُمَّ قِنِي عَذَابَكَ يَوْمَ تَجْمَعُ عِبَادَكَ أَوْ تَبْعَثُ عِبَادَكَ».

O Allah, protect me from Your punishment on the Day You resurrect or gather together Your slaves.
To be read three times when you lie down, placing your right hand under your right cheek.[203]

6. In <u>S</u>a<u>h</u>ee<u>h</u> Muslim :

«اللَّهُمَّ رَبَّ السَّمْوَاتِ وَرَبَّ الأَرْضِ وَرَبَّ الْعَرْشِ الْعَظِيمِ،
رَبَّنَا وَرَبَّ كُلِّ شَيْءٍ، فَالِقَ الْحَبِّ وَالنَّوَىٰ، وَمُنْزِلَ التَّوْرَاةِ
وَالْإِنْجِيلِ، وَالْفُرْقَانِ، أَعُوذُ بِكَ مِنْ شَرِّ كُلِّ شَيْءٍ أَنْتَ آخِذٌ
بِنَاصِيَتِهِ. اللَّهُمَّ أَنْتَ الأَوَّلُ فَلَيْسَ قَبْلَكَ شَيْءٌ، وَأَنْتَ الآخِرُ
فَلَيْسَ بَعْدَكَ شَيْءٌ، وَأَنْتَ الظَّاهِرُ فَلَيْسَ فَوْقَكَ شَيْءٌ، وَأَنْتَ
الْبَاطِنُ فَلَيْسَ دُونَكَ شَيْءٌ، اقْضِ عَنَّا الدَّيْنَ وَأَغْنِنَا مِنَ الْفَقْرِ».

*O Allah, Lord of the heavens and the earth and Lord of
the exalted throne, our Lord and Lord of all things.*

*Splitter of the seed and the date stone and the Revealer
of the Tawraah, the Injeel and the Furqaan. I seek
refuge in You from the evil of all things You shall
seize by the forelock.*[1]

*O Allah, You are the First, and there is nothing before
You. You are the Last, and there is nothing after You.
You are Adh-Dhaahir, there is nothing above You and
Your are Al-Baatin, there is nothing closer than You.*

*Settle for us our debt and spare us from poverty.*²⁰⁴

7. In <u>S</u>a<u>h</u>ee<u>h</u> Muslim :

«الْحَمْدُ للهِ الَّذِي أَطْعَمَنَا وَسَقَانَا، وَكَفَانَا، وَآوَانَا، فَكُمْ مِمَّنْ
لَا كَافِيَ لَهُ وَلَا مُؤْوِيَ».

*All praise is for Allah, Who fed us and gave us drink
and Who is sufficient for us and has sheltered us. How*

---

[1] i.e. those things that You have total control over.

many are there that have none to suffice them or shelter them?[205]

8. From *Saheeh* Al-Bukharee and *Muslim*:

«سُبْحَانَ اللهِ» (ثَلَاثاو ثَلَاثِين مرة)

Far removed is Allah from any imperfections.(Thirty-three times)

«الْحَمْدُ للهِ» (ثَلَاثاو ثَلَاثِين مرة)

All praise is for Allah. (Thirty-three times)

«اللهُ أَكْبَرُ» (ثَلَاثاو ثَلَاثِين مرة)

Allah is the Greatest. (Thirty-three times)[206]

From the etiquettes of going to sleep, we should:

1. Be in a state of purity, from the *Hadeeth*:

If you come to your bed (i.e. go to sleep), then perform Wudoo'.[207]

2. Sleep on our right side:

... then lie down on your right side.[208]

3. Place the right hand under the right cheek:

When he (ﷺ) went to sleep, he placed his right hand under his right cheek...[209]

4. Dust the bed:

When one of you goes to bed, let him dust the bed because he does not know what comes into it before or after him.[210]

5. Recite *Soorah Al-Kaafiroon*:

$$\text{﴿قُلْ يَـٰٓأَيُّهَا ٱلْكَـٰفِرُونَ﴾}$$

"Say : 'O you disbelievers...'"

(Al-Kaafiroon, 109 : 1 - 6)

From its benefits:

It frees the person from Shirk.[211]

Imam An-Nawawee said:

> *One should perform all that has been mentioned in this Chapter. If he is unable to, then he should do as much as he can from the most important supplications mentioned.*

People sleep during the day as well as the night; therefore, it is possible at those times to fulfill all of these *Sunan*, or at least some of them, twice, as these *Sunan* are not specific to sleeping at night.

On the contrary, these *Sunan* also include the sleep of the day, as the narrations are general.

Benefits of these *Sunan* when going to sleep:

☐ If the Muslim preserves these *Adhkaar* before sleeping, one hundred good deeds will be recorded for him:

> *Every Tasbeeh is Sadaqah, every Takbeer is Sadaqah, every Tahmeed is Sadaqah and every Tahleel is Sadaqah.*[212]

Imaam An-Nawawee said a person gains the reward as if he has paid this amount in charity.

☐ If a Muslim preserves the practice of these supplications before sleeping, one hundred trees will be planted for him, in Paradise:

The Messenger of Allah (ﷺ) passed by Aboo Hurayrah (ﷺ) while he was planting something and said:

'O Aboo Hurayrah, shall I not show you a planting better than this?'

He said:'Of course, O Messenger of Allah'.

He (ﷺ) said: 'Say:..

«سُبْحَانَ اللهِ، وَالْحَمْدُ للهِ، وَلَا إِلَهَ إِلَّا اللهُ، وَاللهُ أَكْبَرُ».

... subhaan allaah, al-hamdu lillaah, laa ilaaha illallaah, al,laahu akbar...

... and a tree will be planted for you in Paradise for every one you say'.[213]

☐ Allah protects His Servant and distances the *Shaytaan* from him for that night and he is kept safe from evil and harm.

☐ The servant ends his day in the remembrance of Allah, in obedience to Him, with trust on Him, seeking help from Him and affirming His Oneness.

CONCLUSION

This is what has been made easy in this compilation of the daily *Sunan*. We ask Allah to allow us to lives according to the *Sunnah* of the Messenger Muhammad (ﷺ) and to die on them.

And our last call is all praises and thanks are for Allah, the Lord of the Worlds.

GLOSSARY OF TERMS

Aayaat	Plural of *Aayah*.
Aayah	In this context, a Verse of the Qur'an. See also: *Kursee, Aayah al-*
Adhaan	The Call to Prayer.
Adhkaar	Plural of *Dhikr*.
Ahaadeeth	Plural of *Hadeeth*.
Asbaat Al-	The offspring of the twelve sons of Prophet Ya'qoob.
'Asr, Salaah al-	The compulsory afternoon prayer.
Baatin, Al-	A Name of Allah that indicates His Awareness and Knowledge of all secrets and what is in the heart. It also indicates His Closeness and Nearness, in a manner that befits His Majesty.
Basmala	The phrase (*bismillaah ar-rahmaan ar-raheem*). See also: *Tasmiyah*
Dajjaal	The False Messiah who will appear towards the end of time.
Dinar	A type of currency. Also see: dirham.
Dhaahir, Adh-	A Name of Allah that indicates the greatness of His attributes and thereof every single creation in respect to His Greatness and Highness, for He is above all of His Creation, with regard to His Essence and Attributes.
Dhikr	Remembering or mentioning Allah.
Dhuhr, Adh- *Salaah*	The compulsory midday prayer.
Dirham	A type of currency. Also see dinar.
Du'aa	Supplication to Allah.
Duhaa, Salaah ad-	The optional mid-morning prayer.
Dunya	This world; the worldly life
Fadeelah, Al-	A position above the rest of creation.

Fajr, Salaah al-	The compulsory dawn prayer.
Fataawa	Plural of *Fatwaa*.
Fatwaa	Legal ruling.
Furqaan, Al-	One of the names of the Qur'an. It means the Criterion – something that distinguishes between truth and falsehood.
Hadeeth	A narration of a saying, action, approval or description of the Prophet (ﷺ).
Harakaat	These are actions pertaining to movement, like walking and talking. Also see: *Sakanaat*.
Hawaariyyoon, Al-	The Disciples of Jesus
Ihraam, Al- Takbeer	The opening *Takbeer* of the prayer.
Injeel, Al-	The Book revealed to Prophet 'Eesaa.
Iqaamah	The second Call to Prayer, made just before the start of the obligatory prayer.
'Isha, Salaah al-	The compulsory night prayer.
Israafeel	The name of the angel who will blow the horn.
Jalsah	Sitting.
Jannah	Paradise.
Jibraa'eel	The name of the angel in charge of delivering the revelation.
Jinn	A creation of Allah with a free will, made from smokeless fire.
Juz'	A division of the Qur'an, equal to 1/30.
Kalimah Tayyibah	Not only refers to a good word, but also the remembrance of Allah, supplication, *Salaam*, praises, noble character and good manners and actions.
Khushoo'	A state of deep concentration and reflection that should be experienced during the prayer
Kursee, Aayah al-	Verse of the Footstool (2: 225).
Maghrib, Salaah al-	The compulsory sunset prayer.
Mahram	Someone you are prohibited to marry, e.g. uncle or aunt, father or mother etc.
Marfoo'	A *Hadeeth* that has been attributed to the Prophet ﷺ.

Masaajid	Plural of *Masjid*.
Mawqoof	A H̲adeeth that has been attributed to a Companion of the Prophet (ﷺ) and not to the Prophet (ﷺ) himself.
Meekaa'eel	The name of the angel in charge of the rain.
Mu'aqqibaat	In the context of this Book, it means the *Adhkaar* that are said after the obligatory prayers.
Mu'awwidhaat	The last three *Suwar* of the Qur'an: Al-*Ikhlaas̲*, Al-*Falaq* and An-*Naas*.
Mudd	The amount that can be held when two average sized hands are cupped.
Muqaddim, Al-	A Name of Allah that refers to the One who puts forward, and favours from His Creation whomsoever He wills.
Naar	Hell.
Qiblah	The direction of the Ka'bah in Makkah.
Qiyaam	The standing position of the prayer.
Qiyaam Al-Layl	The optional late Night Prayer.
Rak'aat	Plural of *Rak'ah*.
Rak'ah	A unit of prayer.
Rawaatib Sunnah	The twelve highly recommended *Sunnah* prayers.
Rukoo'	The bowing position of prayer.
S̲*adaqaat*	Charity.
Sajdah	The prostrating position of the prayer.
Sakanaat	These are actions not involving movement, like sleeping. Also see: *Harakaat*.
Sakeenah	To move calmly and to shun or keep away from frivolity.
S̲*alah* (Prayer)	The prayer of Muslims that consists of standing, bowing and prostrating, at fixed times during the day and night.
S̲*alaah* (Of Allah)	Allah's S̲*alaah* on His servant is His praising him in the highest of gatherings (i.e. of the angels).
S̲*alah* [On The	

Prophet (ﷺ)]	The Muslims *Salaah on the Prophet* (ﷺ) is to say: Allah, send *Salaah* on Muḥammad and his family, as you sent *Salaah* on Ibraaheem and his family. Verily you are Praised, Majestic. This is called *Salaah Al-Ibraahee-miyyah,* and is one form of sending *Salaah* on the Prophet (ﷺ).
Salaam	See *Tasleem.*
Shahaadah	The testimony of faith.
Sharee'ah	The laws of Islam.
Shayyaṯeen	Plural of *Shayṯaan.*
Shaykh	Title of respect given to a scholar of Islaam or a noble old person.
Shayṯaan	The Arabic name for Satan or any devil (from mankind or the *jinn).*
Shirk	To associate partners with Allah in His Lordship, Worship or Names and Attributes.
Siwaak	A tooth stick.
Soorah	A chapter from the Qur'an.
Sujood	Plural of *Sajdah.*
Sunan	The plural of *Sunnah.*
Sunnah	A saying, action or approval of the Prophet (ﷺ).
Sutrah	Something a person places in front of him when praying.
Suwar	*Plural of Soorah.*
Taḥiyaat Al-Masjid	The optional prayer for greeting the *Masjid* that consists of two *Rak'ah.* It is prayed when you enter the *Masjid* before you sit down, as long as no obligatory prayer is being performed.
Tahjeer	With reference to the congre-gational prayer, it means to be early.
Taḥleel	To say:(*laa ilaaha illallaah*).
Taḥmeed	To say:(*al ḥamdu lillaah*).
Takbeer	To say: (*allaahu akbar*). Also, See:*Iḥraam,Takbeer al-*.
Tarteel	To read the Qur'an aloud, in a slow melodious voice.
Tasbeeḥ	To say: (*subḥaan Allah*).
Tashshahud	The initial supplication in the sitting position of the

	prayer, up to and including _Salaah_ on the Prophet (ﷺ).
Tasleem	The Islamic greeting of (*as-salaamu'alayum*).
Tasleem (Greeting)	The Islamic greeting (*as-salaamu 'alaykum*).
Tasleem (prayer)	The action of turning the head to the right and then left to conclude the prayer, and saying:(*as-salaamu 'alaykum wa ra*h*matullaah*).
Tasmiyah	The phrase (*bismillaah*). Also see: *Basmala*.
Tawraah	The Book revealed to Prophet Moosaa.
Thawb	A long outer garment worn by men.
Ummah	Nation or People
Waleemah	Wedding feast.
Waqaar	To lower the gaze and one's voice and to avoid looking around excessively.
Waseelah, Al-	A station in Paradise.
Wudoo'	Ablution.
Yanfuth	A type of blowing used with certain *Adhkaar*, which produces little spit, but more air.

HADEETH REFERENCES

1. *Al-Bukhaaree*, The Book Of Ablution, Hadeeth 183.
2. *Al-Bukhaaree*, The Book Of Invocations, Hadeeth 6312.
3. *Al-Bukhaaree*, The Book Of ablution, Hadeeth 245. *Muslim*, The Book Of Purification, Hadeeth 255.
4. *Al-Bukhaaree*, The Book Of The Beginning Of Creation, Hadeeth 3295. *Muslim*, The Book Of Purification, Hadeeth 245. The wording is according to Muslim.
5. *Muslim*, The Book Of Purification, Hadeeth 278.
6. *Al-Bukhaaree*, The Book Of Ablution, Hadeeth 142. *Muslim*, The Book Of Menstruation, Hadeeth 375.
7. *Aboo Daawood*, The Book Of Purification, Hadeeth 30. *At-Tirmidhee*, The Book Of Purification, Hadeeth.
7. *Ibn Maajah*, The Book Of Purification And Its *Sunan*, Hadeeth 300.
8. *Aboo Daawood*, The Book Of Purification, Hadeeth 101. *At-Tirmidhee*, The Book Of Purification, Hadeeth 25. *Ibn Maajah*, The Book Of Purification And Its *Sunan*, Hadeeth 397.
9. *Al-Bukhaaree*, The Book Of Ablution, Hadeeth 164. *Muslim*, The Book Of Purification, Hadeeth 226. *Zaad Al-Ma'aad*, The Way Of The Prophet (ﷺ) In Ablution.
10. *Aboo Daawood*, The Book Of Fasting, Hadeeth 2366. *At-Tirmidhee*, The Book Of Fasting, Hadeeth 788. *An-Nasaaee'*, The Book Of Purification, Hadeeth 87. *Ibn Maajah*, The Book Of Purification And Its *Sunan*, Hadeeth 407.

11. *Al-Bukhaaree*, The Book Of Ablution, Hadeeth 191.
    Muslim, The Book Of Purification, Hadeeth 235.
12. *Musnad Imaam Ahmad*, The Remaining *Musnand* Of Those People Who Have Narrated Many *Ahaadeeth*, Hadeeth 9928.
13. *At-Tirmidhee*, The Book Of Purification, Hadeeth 31.
14. *Al-Bukhaaree*, The Book Of Ablution, Hadeeth 185.
    Muslim, The Book Of Purification, Hadeeth 235.
15. *Aboo Daawood*, The Book Of Fasting, Hadeeth 142.
    At-Tirmidhee, The Book Of Fasting, Hadeeth 788.
    An-Nasaaee', The Book Of Purification, Hadeeth 114. *Ibn Maajah*, The Book Of Purification And Its *Sunan*, Hadeeth 448.
16. *Al-Bukhaaree*, The Book Of Ablution, Hadeeth 168.
    Muslim, The Book Of Purification, Hadeeth 268.
    The wording according to *Al-Bukhaaree*.
17. *Al-Bukhaaree*, The Book Of Ablution, Hadeeth 159.
    Muslim, The Book Of Purification, Hadeeth 226.
18. *Muslim*, The Book Of Purification, Hadeeth 234.
19. *Muslim*, the Book Of *Masaajid* And Places To Pray, Hadeeth 666.
20. *Ibn Khuzaymah*, The Book Of Ablution, Hadeeth 118.
21. *Al-Bukhaaree*, The Book Of Ablution, Hadeeth 201.
    Muslim, the Book Of Purification Hadeeth 325.
22. *Muslim*, The Book Of Purification Hadeeth 246.
23. *Al-Bukhaaree*, The Book Of Ablution, Hadeeth 159.
    Muslim, The Book Of Purification Hadeeth 226.
24. *Muslim*, The Book Of Purification Hadeeth 234.
25. *Muslim*, The Book Of Purification Hadeeth 245.

26. *Muslim*, The Book Of Purification <u>H</u>adeeth 234.
27. *Al-Bukhaaree*, The Book Of Friday, <u>H</u>adeeth 887.
     Muslim, The Book Of Purification <u>H</u>adeeth 252.
28. *Muslim*, The Book Of Purification <u>H</u>adeeth 253.
29. *Al-Bukhaaree*, The Book Of Ablution, <u>H</u>adeeth 245.
     Muslim, The Book Of Purification <u>H</u>adeeth 255.
30. *Musnad Imaam A<u>h</u>mad, Musnad* Of The Ten People Who Were Given The Glad Tidings Of Paradise, <u>H</u>adeeth 7.
31. *Muslim*, The Book Of Clothing and Beautification, <u>H</u>adeeth 2096.
32. *Aboo Daawood*, The Book Of Clothing, <u>H</u>adeeth 4023.
33. *Aboo Daawood*, The Book Of clothing, <u>H</u>adeeth 4141.
     At-Tirmidhee, The Book Of Clothing <u>H</u>adeeth 1765.
     The wording is according to Aboo Daawood.
34. *Muslim*, The Book Of Drinks, <u>H</u>adeeth 2018.
35. *Aboo Daawood*, The Book Of Good Manners, <u>H</u>adeeth 5096.
36. *Muslim*, The Book Of Purification, <u>H</u>adeeth 253.
37. *Aboo Daawood*, The Book Of Good Manners, <u>H</u>adeeth 5095.
     At-Tirmidhee, The Book Of supplications, <u>H</u>adeeth 3426.
38. *Al-Bukhaaree*, The Book Of *Al-Adhaan*, <u>H</u>adeeth 615.
     Muslim, The Book Of Prayer, <u>H</u>adeeth 437.
39. *Muslim*, The Book Of The Prayer The Traveller And Its Shortening, <u>H</u>adeeth 763.
40. *Al-Bukhaaree*, The Book Of *Al-Adhaan*, <u>H</u>adeeth 636.
     Muslim, The Book Of *Masaajid* And Places for Prayer, <u>H</u>adeeth 602.

41. *Muslim*, The Book Of Purification, *Hadeeth* 251.
42. *An-Nasaaee'*, The Book Of *Masaajid*, *Hadeeth* 728.
    Ibn Maajah, The Book Of *Masaajid* And Congregational Prayer, *Hadeeth* 771.
43. *Mustadarak Al-Haakim*, The Book Of The *Imaam*, The Prayer And The Congregation, *Hadeeth* 822.
    He said it is authentic, on the conditions set by Imaam Muslim.
    Adh-Dhahabee agreed with the grading.
44. *Al-Bukhaaree*, The Book Of The Night Prayer, *Hadeeth* 1163.
    Muslim, The Book Of The Prayer Of the Traveller And Its Shortening, *Hadeeth* 714.
45. *Al-Bukhaaree*, The Book Of *Al-Adhaan*, *Hadeeth* 615.
    Muslim, The Book Of Prayer, *Hadeeth* 437.
46. *Muslim*, The Book Of The Prayer Of The Traveller And Its shortening, *Hadeeth* 713.
    Aboo Daawood, The Book Of Prayer, *Hadeeth* 465.
47. *Mustadarak Al-Haakim*, The Book Of The *Imaam*, The Prayer And The congregation, *Hadeeth* 822.
    He said it is authentic, on the conditions set by Imaam Muslim. Adh-Dehahabee agreed with the grading.
48. *Al-Bukhaaree*, The Book Of Prayer, *Hadeeth* 613.
    Muslim, The Book Of Prayer, *Hadeeth* 385. The wording is according to *Muslim*.
49. *Muslim*, The Book Of Prayer, *Hadeeth* 386.
50. *Muslim*, The Book Of Prayer, *Hadeeth* 384.
51. *Al-Bukhaaree*, The Book Of Stories Of the Prophets, *Hadeeth* 3370.

52. *Al-Bukhaaree*, The Book Of *Al-Adhaan*, Hadeeth 614.

53. *Aboo Daawood*, The Book Of Prayer, Hadeeth 524. Al-Haafidh Ibn Hajar graded the Hadeeth as *Hasan* and Ibn Hibbaan gave it a grading of authentic.

54. The Standing Committee For Research And *Fataawa*, 5th Printing, 2003 Volume 6, Book Of Salaah (I), Page 89, *Fatwaa* 2801.

55. The Standing Committee For Research And Fataawa, 5th Printing, 2003, volume 6, Book Of Salaah (I), Page 89, *Fatwaa* 2801 and Page 90, *Fatwaa* 5609.

56. *Aboo Daawood*, The Book Of Prayer, Hadeeth 698. *Ibn Maajah*, The Book Of Establishing The Prayer and Its *Sunan*, Hadeeth 954.

57. *Aboo Daawood*, The Book Of Prayer, Hadeeth 685. *Ibn Maajah*, The Book Of Establishing The Prayer And Its *Sunan*, Hadeeth 945.

58. *Al-Bukhaaree*, The Book Of Prayer, Hadeeth 506.

59. *Aboo Daawood*, The Book Of Prayer, Hadeeth 698.

60. *At-Tirmidhee*, The Book Of Prayer, Hadeeth 335.

61. *Ibn Maajah*, The Book Of Establishing The Prayer And Its *Sunan*, Hadeeth 949.

62. *Muslim*, The Book Of Prayer Of The Traveller And Its Shortening, Hadeeth 728.

63. *Muslim*, The Book Of The Prayer Of The Traveller And Its Shortening, Hadeeth 720.

64. *Al-Bukhaaree*, The Book Of Fasting, Hadeeth 1981. *Muslim*, The Book Of The Prayer Of The Traveller And Its Shortening, Hadeeth 721.

65. *Aboo Daawood*, The Book Of Prayer, Hadeeth 1271.
    At-Tirmidhee, The Book Of Prayer, Hadeeth 430.

66. *Al-Bukhaaree*, The Book Of The Night Prayer, Hadeeth 1183.

67. *Al-Bukhaaree*, The Book Of *Al-Adhaan*, Hadeeth 627.
    Muslim, The Book Of The Prayer Of The Traveller and Its shortening, Hadeeth 304.

68. *Muslim*, The Book Of Fasting, Hadeeth 1163.

69. *Al-Bukhaaree*, The Book Of The Night Prayer, Hadeeth 1138.

70. *Al-Bukhaaree*, The Book Of The Night Prayer, Hadeeth 1138.

71. *Al-Bukhaaree*, The Book Of Ablution, Hadeeth 245.

72. *Al-Bukhaaree*, The Book Of Ablution, Hadeeth 183.
    Muslim, the Book Of The Prayer Of The Traveller and Its Shortening, Hadeeth 763.

73. *Al-Bukhaaree*, The Book Of the Night Prayer, Hadeeth 1120.
    Muslim, The Book Of The Prayer Of The Traveller And Its Shortening, Hadeeth 769. The supplication mentioned is according to the wording of *Al-Bukhaaree*.

74. *Muslim*, The Book Of The Prayer Of The Traveller And Its Shortening, Hadeeth 768.

75. *Muslim*, The Book Of The Prayer Of The Traveller And Its Shortening, Hadeeth 770.

76. *Muslim*, The Book Of The Prayer Of The Traveller And Its Shortening, Hadeeth 756.

77. *Muslim*, The Book Of The Prayer Of The Traveller And Its Shortening, Hadeeth 772.

78. *Aboo Daawood*, The Book Of Prayer, Ḥadeeth 1423 and 1424.

    An-Nasaaee', The Book Of Prayer In the Night And Obedience In The Day, Ḥadeeth 1740.

79. *Aboo Daawood*, The Book Of Prayer, Ḥadeeth 1430. *An-Nasaaee'*, The Book Of Prayer In The Night And Obedience In The Day, Ḥadeeth 1740. Shaykh Al-Arnaut graded these two *Aḥaadeeth* authentic.

80. *Al-Bukhaaree*, The Book Of *Al-Adhaan*, Ḥadeeth 169. *Muslim*, The Book Of The Prayer Of The Traveller And Its Shortening, Ḥadeeth 723.

81. *Muslim*, The Book Of The Prayer Of The Traveller And Its Shortening, Ḥadeeth 727.

82. *Muslim*, The Book Of The Prayer Of The Traveller And Its Shortening, Ḥadeeth 726.

83. *Al-Bukhaaree*, The Book Of The Night Prayer, Ḥadeeth 1160.

84. *Muslim*, The Book Of *Masaajid* And Places For Prayer, Ḥadeeth 670.

85. *Al-Bukhaaree*, The Book Of Prayer, Ḥadeeth 445.

86. *Aboo Daawood*, The Book Of Prayer, Ḥadeeth 776. *At-Tirmidhee*, The Book Of The Opening Supplications, Ḥadeeth 898. *Ibn Maajah*, The Book Of Establishing The Prayer And Its *Sunan*, Ḥadeeth 804.

87. *Al-Bukhaaree*, The Book Of *Al-Adhaan*, Ḥadeeth 744. *Muslim*, The Book Of *Masaajid* And Places For Prayer, Ḥadeeth 598.

88. *Aboo Daawood*, The Book Of Prayer, Ḥadeeth 770.

89. *Muslim*, The Book Of The Opening, Ḥadeeth 399. *An-Nasaaee'*, The Book Of The Opening Ḥadeeth 906.

90. *Al-Bukhaaree*, The Book Of *Al-Adhaan*, Hadeeth 782.

Muslim, The Book Of Prayer, Hadeeth 410.

91. *Al-Bukhaaree*, The Book Of *Al-Adhaan*, Hadeeth 756. *Muslim*, The Book Of Prayer, Hadeeth 394.

92. *Muslim*, The Book Of Prayer, Hadeeth 392.

93. *Muslim*, The Book Of Prayer, Hadeeth 471.

94. *Aboo Daawood*, The Book Of Prayer, Hadeeth 881.

95. *Ibn Maajah*, The Book Of Prayer And The *Sunan* In It, Hadeeth 897.

96. *Al-Bukhaaree*, The Book Of Funerals, Hadeeth 1377. *Muslim*, The Book Of *Masaajid* And Places For Prayer, Hadeeth 588. The wording is according to Muslim.

97. *Muslim*, The Book Of Prayer, Hadeeth 482.

98. *Al-Bukhaaree*, The Book Of *Al-Adhaan*, Hadeeth 736,737 and 738.

Muslim, The Book of Prayer, Hadeeth 390.

99. *Al-Bukhaaree*, The Book Of *Al-Adhaan*, Hadeeth 736,737 and 738.

Muslim, The Book of Prayer, Hadeeth 390.

100. *Al-Bukhaaree*, The Book Of *Al-Adhaan*, Hadeeth 736,737 and 738.

Muslim, The Book of Prayer, Hadeeth 390.

101. *Al-Bukhaaree*, The Book Of *Al-Adhaan*, Hadeeth 739.

102. *Al-Bukhaaree*, (*As-Sunan Al-Kubra*), The Book Of Prayer, Hadeeth 2320.

103. *Al-Bukhaaree*, The Book Of *Al-Adhaan*, Hadeeth 736,737 and 738.

Muslim, The Book of Prayer, Hadeeth 390 and 391.

104. *Al-Bukhaaree*, The Book Of *Al-Adhaan*, Hadeeth 740. *Muslim*, The Book Of Prayer, Hadeeth 401. *Aboo Daawood*, The Book Of Prayer, Hadeeth 755. *Ibn Khuzaymah*, The Book Of Prayer, Hadeeth 479.

105. *Al-Bayhaqee*, The Book Of Hajj, Hadeeth 9726. *Al-Bayhaqee*, The Book Of Salaah, Hadeeth 3543 to 3545.

106. *Muslim*, The Book Of The Prayer, Of The Traveller And Its Shortening, Hadeeth 733.

107. *Aboo Daawood*, The Book Of Prayer, Hadeeth 863. *Mustadarak Al-Haakim*, The Book Of The *Imaam*, The Prayer and The Congregation, Hadeeth 845.

108. Al-Bukhaaree, The Book Of *Al-Adhaan*, Hadeeth 828.

109. *Aboo Daawood*, The Book Of Prayer, Hadeeth 730.

110. *At-Tirmidhee*, The Book Of Prayer, Hadeeth 260.

111. *Al-Bukhaaree*, The Book Of *Al-Adhaan*, Hadeeth 828. *Aboo Daawood*, The Book Of Prayer, Hadeeth 900.

112. *An-Nasaaee'*, The Book Of Performing - The Prayer, Hadeeth 1099 and 1129.

113. *Al-Bukhaaree*, The Book Of *Al-Adhaan*, Hadeeth 828.

114. *Ibn Khuzaymah*, The Book Of Prayer, Hadeeth 654.

115. *Ibn Khuzaymah*, The Book Of Prayer, Hadeeth 641.

116. *Ibn Abee Shaybah*, Volume 1, Chapter 36, Hadeeth 5.

117. *Ibn Khuzaymah*, The Book Of Prayer, Hadeeth 642. *Al-Bayhaqee*, the Book Of Prayer, Hadeeth 419.

118. *Aboo Daawood*, The Book Of Prayer, Hadeeth 732. *Ibn Abee Shaybah*, Volume 1, Chapter 36, Hadeeth 1 to 8.

119. *Muslim*, The Book Of *Masaajid* And Places For Prayer, Hadeeth 536.

120. *Al-Bukhaaree*, The Book Of *Al-Adhaan*, *Hadeeth* 828.

121. *Al-Bukhaaree*, The Book Of *Al-Adhaan*, *Hadeeth* 821.

122. *Al-Bukhaaree*, The Book Of *Al-Adhaan Hadeeth* 824.

123. *Al-Bukhaaree*, The Book Of *Al-Adhaan Hadeeth* 828.

124. *Muslim*, The Book Of *Masaajid* And Places For Prayer, *Hadeeth* 579.

125. *Aboo Daawood*, The Book Of Prayer, *Hadeeth* 731.

126. *Muslim*, The Book Of *Masaajid* And Places For Prayer, *Hadeeth* 579.

127. *Musnad Imaam Ahmad*, The *Musnad* Of Those People Form Amongst The Companions Who Have Narrated Many *Ahaadeeth*, *Hadeeth* 6000.

128. *Aboo Daawood*, The Book Of Prayer, *Hadeeth* 992.

129. *Muslim*. The Book Of *Masaajid* And Places For Prayer, *Hadeeth* 591.

130. Muslim, The Book Of *Masaajid* And Places For Prayer, *Hadeeth* 597.

131. *At-Tirmidhee*, The Book Of Supplications, *Hadeeth* 3534.

132. *At-Tirmidhee*, The Book Of Supplications, *Hadeeth* 3486.

133. *Al-Bukhaaree*, The Book Of *Al-Adhaan*, *Hadeeth* 844. *Muslim*, The Book Of *Masaajid* And Places For Prayer, *Hadeeth* 593.

134. *Muslim*, The Book Of *Masaajid* And Places For Prayer, *Hadeeth* 594.

135. *Aboo Daawood*, The Book Of Prayer *Hadeeth* 1522. *An-Nasaaee'*, The Book Of Prostration Of Forgetfulness, *Hadeeth* 1302.

136. *Al-Bukhaaree*, The Book Of *Jihaad*, *Hadeeth* 2822.
137. *Muslim*, The Book Of The Prayer Of The Traveller And Its Shortening, *Hadeeth* 709.
138. *Aboo Daawood*, The Book Of Good Manners, *Hadeeth* 5082. *At-Tirmidhee*, The Book Of Supplications, *Hadeeth* 3575.
139. *An-Nasaaee'*, *Amal Al-Yawm Wa Al-Laylah*, *Hadeeth* 100.
140. *Saheeh At-Targheeb Wa At-Tarheeb*. The Book Of Prayer, *Hadeeth* 464 to 471.
141. *Muslim*, the Book Of The Prayer Of The Traveller And Its Shortening, *Hadeeth* 720.
142. *Ibn Maajah*, The Book Of Good manners, *Hadeeth* 3807. Shaykh Al-Albaanee graded this narration as authentic.
143. *Saheeh Al-Jaami' As-Sagheer*, *Hadeeth* 6464.
144. *Muslim*, The Book Of *Masaajid* and Places For Prayer, *Hadeeth* 597.
145. *Muslim*, The Book Of *Masaajid* And Places For Prayer, *Hadeeth* 596.
146. *Saheeh Al-Jaami' As-Sagheer*, *Hadeeth* 1194 (or 2571).
147. *Saheeh At-Targheeb Wa At-Tarheeb*, The Book Of Voluntary Deeds, *Hadeeth* 662.
148. *Aboo Daawood*, The Book Of Good Manners, *Hadeeth* 5082. *At-Tirmidhee*, The Book Of Supplications, *Hadeeth* 3575.
149. *Saheeh At-Targheeb Wa At-Tarheeb*, The Book Of Voluntary Deeds, *Hadeeth* 657.
150. *Muslim*, The Book Of Remembrance, supplication, Repentance and Forgiveness, *Hadeeth* 2723.

151. *Aboo Daawood,* The Book Of Good Manners, *Hadeeth* 5068. *At-Tirmidhee,* The Book Of Supplications, *Hadeeth* 3391.

152. *Ibn Maajah,* The Book Of Establishing The Prayer And Its *Sunan, Hadeeth* 925.

153. *At-Tirmidhee,* The Book Of Supplications, *Hadeeth* 3605. *Ibn Maajah,* The Book Of Medicine, *Hadeeth* 3518. *Musnad Imaam Ahmad,* The Remaining *Musnad* Of Those People Who Have Narrated Many *Ahaadeeth, Hadeeth* 8880.

154. *Aboo Daawood,* The Book Of Good Manners, *Hadeeth* 5069 and 5078.

155. *Aboo Daawood,* The Book Of Good Manners, *Hadeeth* 5090, *Musnad Imaam Ahmad,* The First *Musnad* Of The People Of Al-Basra, *Hadeeth* 20430.

156. *Aboo Daawood,* The Book Of Good Manners, *Hadeeth* 5090, *Musnad Imaam Ahmad,* The First *Musnad* Of The People Of Al-Basra, *Hadeeth* 20430.

157. *Al-Bukhaaree,* The Book Of Supplications, *Hadeeth* 6306.

158. *Musnad Imaam Ahmad,* The *Musnad* Of The People Of Makkah, *Hadeeth* 15360.

159. *An-Nasaaee', Amal Al-Yawm Wa Al-Laylah, Hadeeth* 7.

160. *Aboo Daawood,* The Book Of Good Manners, *Hadeeth* 5071. Narrated by *Aboo Daawood Mawqoof.*

161. *Aboo Daawood,* The Book Of Good Manners, *Hadeeth* 5088. *At-Tirmidhee,* The Book Of Supplications, *Hadeeth* 3388. *Ibn Maajah,* The Book Of Supplications, *Hadeeth* 3869.

162. *Aboo Daawood*, The Book Of Good Manners, *Hadeeth* 5072. *At-Tirmidhee*, The Book Of Supplications, *Hadeeth* 3389. *Ibn Maajah*, The Book Of Supplication, *Hadeeth* 3870. *Musnad Imaam Ahmad*, The First *Musnad* Of The People Kufa, *Hadeeth* 18967.

The *Hadeeth* narrated by *Imaam Ahmad* mentions saying the supplication three times in the morning and the evening.

163. *Muslim*, The Book Of Remembrance, Supplication, repentance And Seeking Forgiveness, *Hadeeth* 2702.

164. *Muslim*, The Book Of Remembrance, Supplication, Repentance and Forgiveness, *Hadeeth* 2726.

165. *Muslim*, The Book Of Remembrance, Supplication, Repentance and Forgiveness *Hadeeth* 2692.

166. *Al-Bukhaaree*, The Book Of Supplications, *Hadeeth* 6405.

167. *Al-Bukhaaree*, The Book Of The Beginning Of Creation, *Hadeeth* 3293. *Muslim*, The Book Of Remembrance, Supplication, Repentance and Forgiveness, *Hadeeth* 2691.

168. *Saheeh Al-Kalimaat At-Tayyib*, *Hadeeth* 21.

169. *Al-Bukhaaree*, The Book Of *Eemaan*, *Hadeeth* 12. *Muslim*, The Book Of *Eemaan*, *Hadeeth* 39.

170. *Aboo Daawood*, The Book Of Good Manners, *Muslim*, The Book Of *Eemaan*, *Hadeeth* 5195. *At-Tirmidhee*, The Book Of Asking Permission and Good manners, *Muslim*, The Book Of *Eemaan*, *Hadeeth* 2689.

171. *Aboo Daawood* The Book Of Good Manners, *Muslim*, The Book Of *Eemaan*, Hadeeth 5208. *At-Tirmidhee*, The Book Of Asking Permission And Good Manners, *Muslim*, The Book Of *Eemaan*, Hadeeth 2706.

172. *Muslim*, The Book Of Piety, Joining Of The Ties Of Relationship and Good Manners, *Muslim*, The Book Of *Eemaan*, Hadeeth 2626.

173. *Aboo Daawood*, The Book Of Good Manners, *Muslim*, The Book Of *Eemaan*, Hadeeth 5212. *At-Tirmidhee*, The Book Of Asking Permission And Good Manners, *Muslim*, The Book Of *Eemaan*, Hadeeth 2727.

174. *Al-Bukhaaree*, The Book Of *Jihaad*, Hadeeth 2989. *Muslim*, The Book Of *Az-Zakaah*, Hadeeth 1009.

175. *Muslim*, The Book Of Drinks, Hadeeth 2022.

176. *Muslim*, *The Book Of Drinks*, Hadeeth 2034.

177. *Muslim*, The Book Of Drinks, Hadeeth 2032.

178. *Muslim*, The Book Of Drinks, Hadeeth 2033.

179. *Muslim*, The Book Of Drinks, Hadeeth 2734.

180. *At-Tirmidhee*, The Book Of Supplications, Hadeeth 3458. *Ibn Maajah*, The Book of Food, Hadeeth 3285. *Shaykh Al-Albaanee* graded the narration as good.

181. *Muslim*, The Book Of Drinks, Hadeeth 2022.

182. *Abu Daawood*, the Book Of Drinks, Hadeeth 3727.

183. *Muslim*, The Book Of Drinks, Hadeeth 2026.

184. *Muslim*, The Book Of Drinks, Hadeeth 2734.

185. *Al-Bukhaaree*, The Book Of *Al-Adhaan*, Hadeeth 731. *Muslim*, The Book Of The Prayer Of The Traveller And Its Shortening Hadeeth 781.

186. *Musnad Aboo Ya'laa*, Hadeeth 3821. *Shaykh Al-Albaanee* graded this narration as authentic.
187. *Saheeh At-Targheeb Wa At-Tarheeb*, The Book Of Desiring To Pray The Voluntary Prayers In The House, Hadeeth 438. Shaykh Al-Albaanee graded this narration as *Hasan*.
188. *Aboo Daawood*, The Book Of Good Manners, Hadeeth 4859. *At-Tirmidhee*, The Book Of Supplications, Hadeeth 3433.
189. *Al-Bukhaaree*, The Book Of The Beginning Of Revelation, Hadeeth 1. *Muslim*, The Book Of Government, Hadeeth 1908.
190. *Aboo Daawood*, The Book Of Prayer, Hadeeth 1516. *At-Tirmidhee*, The Book Of Supplications, Hadeeth 3434.
191. *Muslim*, The Book Of Purification, Hadeeth 373.
192. *At-Tabaraanee*, *Al-Awsat*, Hadeeth 6319. *Al-Bayhaqee*, *Shu'bah Al-Eemaan*, The Chapter Of Belief In Allaah, Hadeeth 119. Shaykh Al-Albaanee graded this narration as *Hasan*.
193. *At-Tirmidhee*, The Book Of Supplications, Hadeeth 3431. *At-Tirmidhee* said this narration is good.
194. *Aboo Daawood*, The Book Of Prayer, Hadeeth 1389.
195. *Al-Bukhaaree*, The Book Of Supplication, Hadeeth 6324.
196. *Al-Bukhaaree*, The Book Of The Virtues Of The Qur'an, Hadeeth 5017.
197. *Al-Bukhaaree*, The Book Of The Virtues Of The Qur'an, Hadeeth 5009.
198. *Al-Bukhaaree*, The Book Of The Virtues Of The Qur'an, Hadeeth 5010.

199. *Al-Bukhaaree*, The Book Of Supplications, Hadeeth 6320. *Muslim*, The Book Of Remembrance, Supplication, Repentance and Forgiveness, Hadeeth 2714.

200. Saheeh Al-Kalimaat At-Tayyib, Hadeeth 21.

201. *Al-Bukhaaree*, The Book Of Supplications, Hadeeth 6313.
   Muslim, The Book Of Remembrance, Supplication, Repentance and Forgiveness, Hadeeth 2710.

202. *Muslim*, The Book Of Remembrance, Supplication, repentance and Forgiveness, Hadeeth 2712.

203. *Aboo Daawood*, The Book Of Good Manners, Hadeeth 5045. *At-Tirmidhee*, The Book Of Supplications, Hadeeth 3398.

204. *Muslim*, the Book Of Remembrance, Supplication, Repentance and Forgiveness, Hadeeth 2713.

205. *Muslim*, The Book Of Supplications, Repentance and Forgiveness, Hadeeth 2715.

206. *Al-Bukhaaree*, The Book Of Supplications, Hadeeth 6318. *Muslim*, The Book Of Remembrance, Supplication, repentance and Forgiveness, Hadeeth 2727 and 2728.

207. *Al-Bukhaaree*, The Book Of Supplications, Hadeeth 6311. *Muslim*, The Book Of Remembrance, Supplication, repentance and Forgiveness, Hadeeth 2710.

208. *Al-Bukhaaree*, The Book Of Supplications, Hadeeth 6311. *Muslim*, The Book Of Remembrance, Supplication, repentance and Forgiveness, Hadeeth 2710.

209. *Al-Bukhaaree*, The Book Of Supplications, *Hadeeth* 6314. *Muslim*, The Book Of Remembrance, Supplication, repentance and Forgiveness, *Hadeeth* 5045.
210. *Al-Bukhaaree*, The Book Of Supplications, *Hadeeth* 6320. *Muslim*, The Book Of Remembrance, Supplication, repentance and Forgiveness, *Hadeeth* 2714.
211. *Aboo Daawood*, The Book Of Good Manners, *Hadeeth* 5055. *At-Tirmidhee*, The Book Of Supplications, *Hadeeth* 3403. *Musnad Imaam Ahmad*, The remaining *Musnad* Of The People Form *Al-Ansaar*, *Hadeeth* 23807. *Mustadarak Al-Haakikm*, The Book Of The Virtues Of The Qur'an *Hadeeth* 2121. Al-Haakim graded this narration as authentic and likewise Adh-Dhahabee. Al-Haafidh Ibn Hajar graded it as good and Shaykh Al-Albaanee graded it authentic.
212. *Muslim*, The Book Of The Prayer Of The Traveller And Its Shortening, *Hadeeth* 720.
213. *Ibn Maajah*, The Book Of Good Manners, *Hadeeth* 3807. *Shaykh Al-Albaanee* graded this narration as authentic.